MW01275710

Traditions, Standards,
& Transformations

PETER LANG
New York • Washington, D.C./Baltimore • Bern
Frankfurt am Main • Berlin • Brussels • Vienna • Oxford

Traditions, Standards, & Transformations

A MODEL FOR PROFESSIONAL DEVELOPMENT SCHOOL NETWORKS

EDITED BY

Jane E. Neapolitan, Thomas D. Proffitt,
Cheryl L. Wittmann, Terry R. Berkeley

PETER LANG
New York • Washington, D.C./Baltimore • Bern
Frankfurt am Main • Berlin • Brussels • Vienna • Oxford

Library of Congress Cataloging-in-Publication Data

Traditions, standards, and transformations: a model for professional
development school networks / edited by Jane E. Neapolitan ... [et al.].
p. cm.
Includes bibliographical references and index.
1. Laboratory schools—Maryland—Case studies. 2. Teachers—
Training of—Maryland—Case studies. 3. College-school cooperation—
Maryland—Case studies. 4. Towson Professional Development
School Network. I. Neapolitan, Jane E.
LB2154.A3T73   370'.71'1—dc22   2003025890
ISBN 0-8204-7250-6

Bibliographic information published by **Die Deutsche Bibliothek**.
Die Deutsche Bibliothek lists this publication in the "Deutsche
Nationalbibliografie"; detailed bibliographic data is available
on the Internet at http://dnb.ddb.de/.

Cover design by Lisa Barfield

© 2004 Peter Lang Publishing, Inc., New York
275 Seventh Avenue, 28th Floor, New York, NY 10001
www.peterlangusa.com

Contents

Foreword

Terry R. Berkeley

This is the first book of a three-volume series about the professional development school partnership. The professional development school (PDS), in some respects, is an educational advance as old as the rural American one-room schoolhouse, an outgrowth of the more recent approach to the professional preparation of teachers known as microteaching, and current enough to take advantage of new policies, advanced technologies, research about brain function, and the relationship of all of this to learning. The PDS is a symbol of how systemic change can be brought to bear to assure the highest level of learning during a time when strict accountability requires the best possible teaching of our nation's children. Towson University is a national leader in the preparation of new teachers and the ongoing professional development of practicing educational professionals because of the forcefulness of the college's desire for respectful, reciprocal partnerships between the university and its faculty and staff, Maryland's public schools, and the statewide cadre of educational professionals.

In this Foreword appreciation is expressed to Dennis Hinkle, the late dean of Towson's College of Education. His leadership in prompting, provoking, and assuring the university's commitment to the highest levels of excellence in the professional development schools movement, his vision, has resulted in the expansion of the scope and reach of Towson's efforts to provide an ever-increasing corps of highly effective educational professionals dedicated to students in the schools, public schools, their learning and other achievements. Simply put, Dennis Hinkle's desire has been for "every student" at Towson and in the public schools to "grow and blossom into the flower of their own potential." (Wooden, 1976, p. 248) He demonstrated this commitment to children and to schooling when serving as dean in the service he gave weekly in a Baltimore County public school as a teacher assistant as well as in all of his other professional and personal efforts. Dennis Hinkle was well known across the nation for his dedication, determination, and devotion in this regard.

The "question" to focus on in this book is just what have Dennis Hinkle, the faculty in the College of Education, and personnel in Towson's partner schools done in the design and development of the PDS, the professional development school? How was such a concerted effort among so many manifested with a resulting deep cultural change between and among partners, the "state," the public schools, and the university, whose past efforts often were unappreciated by one another?

To begin, much of what has been done has to do with the resourcefulness, the personality, the quirks, and the resilience of all involved! Taken together, as will be seen in the work of the authors of the chapters throughout this book, this has resulted in an amassing of effort, assuring that Towson, Maryland's public school districts and communities and Maryland state officials stay at the forefront of teacher training and teacher and school renewal.

Tangibly and intangibly, is there "something" that made all of this effort in time and resources coalesce in such a positive manner? And if there is, what can it be? Perhaps, it is a feeling for and about community.

Community is the place where a school is located. From a historical perspective Butterworth (1926) wrote about the importance of place in the life of a school, particularly rural schools where community is an important force. Three-quarters of a century after Butterworth, the same holds true. Often, though, we forget about community in what it is that we do. Until the recent focus of attention on service learning, the value and importance of community typically have been overlooked in the professional preparation of teachers. One might speculate as to why the importance of community has been left out of the equation of schools and schooling during this time of calls for stringent accountability through high stakes testing. Perhaps, community is supposed to be thought of as merely a natural ingredient of our collective conscience in America. Unless community is nurtured, just as schools must be nurtured, there can be only limited value for both schools and community.

What, then, is community? Simply, Lemke writes "community [is being] part of a group of people with whom you have something in common. There is a sense of unity and common ground" (p. 3). This does not mean everyone gets along in idyllic harmony. Rather, there is an understanding of place and the fit of people into that place "with a key distinction often being the sense of common good outweighing the broad spectrum of difference" (Smith, Berkeley, Lemke & Ryan, 2001, p. 4)

If community is to be a positive force in the preparation of teachers, and in this case through the professional development school partnership, caring should be at the center of all we do together "in unity and (on a) common ground." In short, this may have to do with wanting the best for all those who are a part of the PDS partnership. This includes the students enrolled in the schools, the parents of those children, the faculty, staff, and administrators working in the schools, the university students or interns, and the university faculty, staff, and administrators. Inherently, this means the citizens who live in a community. Noddings (1999) discusses how care and caring can be considered among the parties to the PDS partnership asking, "What happens now to relationships? What happens to communities? What happens to the quality of experience for those who will undergo the consequences of our decisions [to create a PDS partnership]?" (p. 12) "Caring," then, she notes, "refers properly to the relation[ship], not just to an agent who cares, we must consider the response of the cared-for." (p. 13)

In the professional development school partnerships described in this book, there is a significant focus on care, the cared-for, caring, and community. The systemic change brought about by the parties to these PDS partnerships could only have occurred with a commitment to caring by those who are caring as well as the cared-for who return that care (Noddings, 1992). The result? A community of learners in respectful exchange moving to the ideal of doing good and doing good well.

References

Butterworth, J.E. (1926). *Rural school administration.* New York: Macmillan.

Noddings, N. (1992). *Caring: A feminine approach to ethics & moral education.* Berkeley: University of California Press.

Noddings, N. (1999). Care, justice, and equity. In M.S. Katz, N. Noddings, & K.A. Strike (Eds.), *Justice and caring: The search for common ground in education* (pp. 7–20). New York: Teachers College Press.

Smith, D.J., Berkeley, T.R., Lemke, J., & Ryan, S.M. (2001). Prologue: Rural: Was it ever really the farm? *Rural Special Education Quarterly, 20,* 3–5.

Wooden, K. (1976), *Weeping in the playtime of others: America's incarcerated children.* New York: McGraw-Hill.

Acknowledgments

This book was developed and written as a result of a unique collective of professional dedication and personal support. Each of the editors has their own story about coming to the work they do in professional development school partnerships. We feel great good fortune in being able to collaborate with so many of our professional colleagues and friends! We are most appreciative to all of those in our personal lives who have reinforced the work we do on an ongoing basis, especially when it takes up so much time.

Professionally, we would like to thank each person with whom we have met, each person with whom we have collaborated, on this journey of the past 10 years. We are especially indebted to Dr. Nancy Grasmick, superintendent of schools in the Maryland State Department of Education (MSDE) and the entire Program Approval and Assessment Branch, led by Dr. Virginia Pilato. MSDE has been so helpful in providing financial resources and great encouragement to Towson's Institute for Professional Development School Studies, allowing us to examine the PDS from so many different perspectives for so long a period of time. In addition, we are appreciative of all of our College of Education colleagues for their candor and other support to provide the best of themselves to our students and to students in the public schools with whom we collaborate. All we have done has been accomplished through the collective will of so many.

We would like to thank Ms. Linda Caldwell, administrative assistant in Towson's Department of Early Childhood Education for her effort in assuring this book was prepared in camera-ready copy for the publisher. And for doing so under incredibly tight time constraints. Acknowledgments and thanks are not nearly enough for all that she has done!

Personally, we would like to acknowledge our appreciation and dedicate this book to those in our lives who prompted us to accomplish our best:

For JEN: To Michael, Andy, Chris, Tony, Olinda, and Lorraine.
For TDP: To Kathy, Kristin, and Kelly.
For CLW: To Bob, Frankie, Wanda, and Lois.
For TRB: To Suzanne, Anna, Jason, Kris, and Wes.

PART ONE

Building on Traditions

CHAPTER ONE

History and Development of the Towson Professional Development School Network

Thomas D. Proffitt, Maggie Madden,
Cheryl L. Wittmann & Teresa T. Field

In this chapter the history, development, and institutionalization of "A Community of Learners," the Towson Professional Development School Network, are chronicled. Initiated in 1994 at a single site in one school district, the network now encompasses more than 80 schools in nine school districts in the metropolitan Baltimore and Washington DC regions. While expanding during the past eight years, the network has achieved a state and national reputation. Identified in 1997 by the Maryland State Department of Education as a "state leader in PDS" (MSDE, 1997), the network was recognized nationally in 1998 by the Association of Teacher Educators (ATE) as a "Distinguished Program in Teacher Education." Subsequently, the network was selected by the National Council for Accreditation of Teacher Education (NCATE) as one of the 19 sites throughout the nation to conduct a three-year pilot (1997–2000) of the NCATE Standards for Professional Development Schools (PDS). In 2001, continuing its commitment to expanding the knowledge base about PDS standards and implementation, a Towson PDS was selected as one of four sites to field test the recently developed Maryland PDS Standards. These state and national recognitions reinforce Towson's efforts in the simultaneous renewal of P–12 schools and teacher education programs, thus reflecting the truly collaborative nature of partnerships within the network.

National and State Context

In the last two decades, from *A Nation at Risk* (1983) to *What Matters Most: Teaching for America's Future* (1996) to *Investing in Teaching* (2001), renewal, redesign, restructure, and reform have become the agenda for P–12 schools and higher education institutions, specifically in teacher education. As these efforts have progressed, the expectation of simultaneous renewal/reform has become apparent along with the need for extended collaborations between the two types of institutions. Promoted by a range of organizations, these extended collaborations have taken on a variety of names, e.g., clinical schools (Carnegie, 1986), professional practice schools (Levine, 1988), and more recently, professional development schools (Holmes Group, 1986, 1990, 1995; Darling-Hammond, 1994). By any name, these P–16 partnerships have been created to initiate and sustain the simultaneous renewal/reform of P–12 and teacher education as well as to provide for the continuous professional development of educators from pre-service, through induction, and throughout their professional careers.

In the most recent attempt to transform the context for the preparation of teacher candidates and continuous professional development of experienced teachers, the professional development school has become the cornerstone of evolving programs. Noting their potential to reinvent teacher education, the National Commission on Teaching and America's Future (1996) identified among the strengths of PDSs the focus on simultaneous renewal of P–16 institutions, extended clinical training through a coherent program of mentoring and instruction by school and university faculty, and the integration of theory and practice (thereby correcting this long-standing fragmentation), and reconnecting P–16 education, especially on school sites.

A broad body of literature has developed that describes the principles, beliefs, goals, characteristics, and effectiveness of PDS (Book, 1996; Teitel, 1998, 2001b; Abdul-Haqq, 1998; Clark, 1999). Although this body of literature ranges in quality and focus, there is much consensus around the major goals of a PDS. As summarized by Darling-Hammond (1994),

> PDSs aim to provide new models of teacher education and development by serving as exemplars of practice, builders of knowledge, and vehicles for communicating professional understanding among teacher-educators, novices, and veteran teachers. They support the learning of prospective teachers and beginning teachers by creating settings in which novices enter professional practice by working with expert practitioners, enabling veteran teachers to renew their professional development and assume new roles as mentors, university adjuncts, and teacher leaders. They allow school and university educators to engage jointly in research and rethinking of practice, thus creating an opportunity for the profession to expand its knowledge base by putting research into practice—and practice into research. (p. 1)

One other common focus has emerged from the literature. These new education goals act as a call for substantive changes to be made in the structure and organization of teacher education and K–12 schools. Cuban (1988) noted these changes must be more than shoring up existing structures, what he identified as "first order change"; instead, these changes must be "second order change," those which result in the creation of new structures to support the implementation of the new goals. As the literature confirms, the substantive restructuring of PreK–12 education and teacher education is a complex and arduous task, necessitating the transformation of the cultures and structures of dissimilar institutions.

In Maryland, a major focus of educators and policy makers in the aggressive *Redesign of Teacher Education* (Maryland Higher Education Commission, 1995) has been to create professional development schools. In fact, Maryland's teacher education reform initiative, engendered by the Higher Education Commission (MHEC) and the Maryland State Department of Education (MSDE), made specific reference to professional development schools as the "cornerstone" of the reform agenda (MHEC, 1995).

> The State of Maryland has initiated a number of school reform initiatives. In order for these reforms to be successful, teachers will need to understand and contribute to them. Beginning teachers who enter the school familiar with and committed to these reforms will contribute immediately to the progress and success of the reform effort....The clinical preparation of interns in schools that are fully engaged in school reform will allow them to learn and practice reform simultaneously with practicing teachers. (p. 24)

Thus, the College of Education at Towson University requires all of its teacher candidates to be engaged in an extensive and intensive internship in a professional development school. For an institution such as Towson, which produces the largest number of teachers in the state, in excess of 450 annually, this could seem to be a daunting task. However, Towson pursued the state-mandated policy seriously and systematically planned for implementation in all departments within the College of Education. Since each PDS was collaboratively developed, each reflects the unique nature of the partners within the College of Education's overarching commitment to the PDS model.

Within this national and state professional and policy context, the Towson University PDS Network developed six primary goals:

1. Create a collaborative culture and governance structure to guide the work of the network.
2. Provide an enhanced pre-service experience through the integration of theory and practice in a clinically based teacher education program.
3. Provide need-based, continuous professional development for in-service teachers and administrators.
4. Provide for inquiry into and refinement of effective practices in teaching learning.
5. Maximize student achievement.
6. Disseminate promising practices and structures to the education community.

These components form the foundation for developing, implementing, and institutionalizing individual PDS sites as well as for developing the original Towson University/Baltimore County Public Schools PDS Network and subsequent networks that include other school systems.

Building a Model: In the Beginning

Drawing from national reports and research studies and building upon a rich tradition of educational collaboration, Towson University and Baltimore County (MD) Public Schools (BCPS) began preliminary discussions in search of ways to build stronger connections between pre-service and in-service education. The genesis of the PDS network began in Fall 1993, in a series of meetings between the university and the school system to search for ways to redesign, fundamentally, the clinical features of pre-service education. These initial efforts focused on the concept of a magnet school for "teachers of teachers," i.e., a faculty and school site that would serve as a model "center for best practices" for pre-service teachers.

The initial efforts to conceptualize a new P–16 model for teacher education received support and gained momentum from the arrival of a new dean in the College of Education, new faculty with PDS experience, and a new superintendent in BCPS. Follow-up meetings were held with additional university and school system representatives. National and local studies also made it increasingly evident that the traditional methods of instruction and organization of P–12 schools were not meeting the needs of children in a changing society. As a result, the discussions were expanded to pursue the issue of simultaneous renewal of P–12 and teacher education through a PDS. Both partners' willingness to look at schools and colleges of education through a different lens allowed these initial discussions to be successful.

A PDS Leadership Team was formed to begin formulating a common understanding of the PDS concept and the processes needed to develop the Towson University/BCPS partnership. Members of the team represented Towson faculty and administration, BCPS administrators from the Office of Human Resources and Professional Development, and, once identified (January 6, 1994), the principal and other representatives from Owings Mills Elementary School, the first PDS site and magnet school for "teachers of teachers." This partnership would provide opportunities to link theory and practice *and* assist in developing a pool of new, highly qualified teachers well trained in BCPS curriculum, standards, and procedures to fill an increasing number of vacancies.

Guided by the work of American Association of Colleges of Teacher Education (AACTE), the Benedum Project at West Virginia University, the University of Louisville, and The Holmes Group, the theme of the professional development school, "A Community of Learners," became evident and was operationalized when the PDS model was initiated at Owings Mills Elementary School with the 1994 Summer Strategic Planning Institute. From the outset, the central purpose was to improve teaching and learning for P–16 students, to provide an enhanced pre-service experience built around performance-based standards, and a simultaneous focus on continuous professional development for in-service teachers, being at the core of the Towson PDS model.

A weeklong summer strategic planning institute provided opportunities for teachers, university faculty, parents, pre-service teachers, and other partners to develop a common P-16 mission and vision for the Towson University/Owings Mills Elementary PDS. Once the vision was specified, action plans were developed with specific steps outlined to make the vision a reality. Stakeholders worked together to develop timelines, evaluation procedures, and data collection plans. The "ownership" for these goals was shared by all stakeholders, providing for authentic forms of collaboration and problem solving. Thus, interdependence is critical to an organization seeking to restructure organizational strategies in the public schools and in higher education.

In Fall 1994, the PDS began at Owings Mills Elementary School. This new organization, the Towson University/Owings Mills Elementary School Professional Development School, provided learning opportunities for all in the school community. A classroom at the school became Towson University's "Owings Mills Campus," where pre-service teachers, in-service teachers, and university faculty learned from each other. In a redesigned, quantitatively and qualitatively different clinical experience, Towson juniors and seniors completed coursework and extensive internship experiences at the school, collaboratively mentored by university and school faculty. This "immersion" experience provided more time and more planned and purposeful integrated experiences in the totality of an authentic school culture—in the classroom with students and teachers foremost, and in faculty meetings, parent conferences, school improvement team meetings, and professional development activities.

University faculty had on-site offices and became familiar with the myriad demands on public school personnel, thus ensuring the relevancy and currency of their coursework. In-service teachers took advantage of an array of simultaneous professional development activities, including study groups and on-site graduate courses tailored to school improvement needs. Teachers in the school presented lessons, taught courses, and served as mentors for Towson students. Several papers were written, and presentations were made at national conferences by teams consisting of teachers, university faculty, student teachers, parents, and administrators.

Simultaneous renewal involved discussions about staffing, curriculum, standards, accountability, and evaluation at the university and in the school system. New procedures were developed for creating budgets, for identifying funding, and for allocating and reallocating funds to support tuition remission for in-service teachers. The school calendar was changed allowing Towson students to coincide their schedules more closely with the public school schedule. The teacher education curriculum was revised to meet the needs of students at the school. Specific benchmarks were identified. Data were gathered to determine the viability and effectiveness of the PDS model.

Establishing the Network

Positive outcomes from the Owings Mills partnership, the emergence of Maryland's *Redesign of Teacher Education*, and the availability of new funding sources (including the U.S. Department of Education's Dwight D. Eisenhower Professional Development State Grants Program and Goals 2000 Grant Program) provided the impetus to expand Towson University's PDS model. (Note: These same funding opportunities also supported the development of PDS sites by other colleges and universities.) In order to facilitate discussion and broaden the "community of learners" concept, Towson University sponsored statewide PDS videoconferences from 1994 to 1996 utilizing the university system's Interactive Video Network. Representatives from higher education institutions and public school systems from across the state, as well as representatives of MSDE, participated in these thematic videoconferences where common issues, policy concerns, and funding and research opportunities were discussed. These initial efforts at collaboration among PDS partnerships from across Maryland and with MSDE (which provided some later funding for the teleconferences) contributed to the development of MSDE's Statewide PDS Network and placed Towson at the forefront of Maryland's PDS efforts. Representatives from Towson were active members of the Maryland PDS Policy Board and PDS Operations Team and made significant contributions to the success of Maryland's PDS initiatives.

From 1995 to 1998, supported by new funding sources aligned with ongoing national and state demands to redesign P–16 teacher education, the Towson PDS Network expanded to 13 schools. Based upon the success of the initial PDS at Owings Mills Elementary School, the university began the ongoing process of entering into additional PDS relationships with the Anne Arundel County, Baltimore County, Baltimore City and Howard County school systems. This process began by repeating the same strategic planning process used in developing the initial PDS partnership. Regardless of the unique characteristics of each new site, the successful processes and procedures from the Owings Mills partnership (e.g., community-wide stakeholders, a commonly held vision, shared governance, true collaboration, specific roles and responsibilities, and strategic planning) were the foundation in the development of the new PDS partnerships. In addition, members of Owings Mills PDS leadership team provided guidance during initial discussions and became part of the strategic planning team for many of the "second generation" PDSs by serving as team leaders in the planning workshops in which the focus was on organizational restructuring. The College of Education became the planning hub for the additional sites, and the network became the interorganizational bridge that encouraged/facilitated what Berry & Catoe (1994) call "organizational learning" and worked to overcome "territorial imperatives"(p. 194).

These efforts successfully changed the nature of existing organizational structures at Towson and with the school partners to create a P–16 community of learners. This was manifested through the development and ongoing work in university-school collaborative governance structures. Recognizing that to build, network, and institutionalize P–16 connectedness required "a whole new set of interorganizational relations advanced by boundary spanners—individuals who are accepted in all institutions and are able to sell and mediate actions" (Berry & Catoe, 1994, p. 200), the Towson/Baltimore County partnership created in 1995–1996 a new, jointly funded role of PDS instructional facilitator. Two boundary spanners were hired. Charged with pursuing and implementing a common vision, the facilitators served as liaisons between the two communities in their capacities as members of Towson's Department of Elementary Education involving teaching courses in the PDS and serving as members of the Office of Professional Development in BCPS.

As the Towson PDS initiative expanded, "networking" individual PDS schools with one another (as well as across all of the PDS partnerships) required a governance structure for planning and implementation, including a coordinated and coherent plan for professional development, resource identification and allocation, and evaluation and assessment strategies (Proffitt, Field, Hinkle, & Pilato, 1996; Field & Barksdale-Ladd, 1994). For the Towson University/BCPS collaboration, a PDS Network Coordinating Council was established during 1995–1996, co-chaired by P–12 and university personnel, comprised of building principals, site-based teacher liaisons, university faculty, the boundary-spanning instructional facilitators, and P–12 professional staff development personnel. It was important to the functioning of the network that coordinating council efforts had to focus beyond structural changes needed to successfully implement and sustain individual site partnerships and to focus on the process of developing the interorganizational structure needed to alter the nature of existing organizational cultures in order to build new and meaningful relationships among all participating education professionals.

As the Towson network expanded to include three school systems, the coordinating council became the model for a variety of other PDS-related governance structures. In each school system, the governance vehicle fulfilled the same coordinating council role, therefore, ensuring each PDS addressed site-specific school improvement needs, the professional development needs of faculty, and the implementation of a school-based teacher education program that met the needs of the school community and of a standards-based teacher education program. Cross-site committee meetings, newsletters, electronic connections, and cross-site visitations all served as communication and networking vehicles for this expanding community of learners. Variations of the PDS instructional facilitator role also were pursued and implemented in other systems, including a jointly funded position with the Howard County (MD) Public Schools.

Professional Development in Practice: Network Opportunities

Since the establishment of the PDS network, governance has been addressed in terms of PDS improvement issues and assessments of the needs of local school systems goals for implementing sustained professional development opportunities. The "highlight" of PDS professional development activities in the Towson/Baltimore County PDS Network were semi-annual, network-wide "PDS Institutes." National and state experts in teacher preparation, curriculum, and instruction were engaged to share their expertise to PDS faculty and administrators, university faculty, and interns.

The national and state consultants addressed collaboratively identified instructional concerns and other topics of interest. These issues included addressing the student achievement gap, developing and using performance based assessment measures, encouraging reflective teaching, using multiple intelligences in instruction, and working collaboratively to develop learning communities. Speakers including Lorraine Monroe (1996), Bette McLeod (1996), Jay McTighe (1997 and 1998), Elyse Eidman-Aadahl (1997), Thomas Armstrong (1997), Pedro Noguera (2000), Michael Fullan (2001), and Andy Hargreaves (2002). The activities demonstrated the mutual commitment of Towson and Baltimore County to the network as well as to the goal of continuous professional development. The institutes also served to enhance and extend the learning community from individual PDSs to the network as a whole.

Reflecting the community-of-learners theme, each daylong institute provided practitioners with the opportunity to share "promising practices" from the school classroom and the university classroom, recognizing and celebrating the "experts" within the network. Follow-up inter- and intra-school classroom visitations and regularly scheduled "teacher chats" extended the institutes' learnings and reflection to P–16 participants within the network. To broaden the impact, practitioners from Towson's PDS partnerships in other school systems, as well as PDSs of neighboring universities, were invited to participate in the institutes. Towson continued to promote PDS networking opportunities by hosting the Maryland Professional Development School Network's National Conference in 1998 and in 2003. The national PDS institutes and conferences provided Towson PDS practitioners the opportunity to share with and learn from PDS colleagues across the state and the nation.

The outcomes of PDS institutes were impressive. The participants received substantive information while interpersonal networking conferred a sense of validation about the meaning of the community of learners, in turn creating opportunities for sharing professional expertise and psychological support beyond the walls of an individual school. The institutes also served to promote the integration of two dissimilar cultures: P–12 and teacher education—into a community of learners sharing "a common vision and operating on the basis of mutual trust and respect" (Hinkle & Proffitt, 1996, p.17).

To meet the varying professional development needs of PDS stakeholders at the school and individual level, numerous additional other professional development activities were begun and supported by the various university-school system coordinating councils. These included site-specific workshops, individual PDS instructional retreats, cross-site forums, grant-funded presentations and participation at professional conferences, mini-grants for technology integration, PDS intervisitations, and a great variety of on-site graduate courses.

Continued Development and National Recognition

Driven by national and local research documenting the positive impact of PDS on the learning of interns and the professional development of practicing teachers and supported by grants[1] targeted at teacher education redesign, a second wave of expansion in the network occurred from 1998 to the present with the network growing to the current 80+ sites in nine school systems. (For Towson PDS impact research, see Altwerger & Cole, 1997; Neubert & Binko, 1998; Yarrison, 1996; Maxwell, Morgan, & Proffitt, 1999; and Richmond, 1998. Simultaneously, demands for national PDS standards and additional accountability and documented results were emerging.

Previously cited as a "state leader in PDS" in its *MSDE Program Approval Visit Report* (1998c, p. 2), the Towson PDS Network applied for and became one of 19 national pilot sites for the National Council for Accreditation of Teacher Education (NCATE) PDS Standards Field-Test Project. After its October 2000 visit, the NCATE summary report provided additional validation for the network. Commending "an environment that simultaneously supports the learning of elementary school students, teacher candidates, school and university faculty, and administrators in an integrated way," it was stated in the report that "support for professional development…has become so deeply embedded in the cultures of both school and university that the two institutions have made significant changes in their practices, procedures, and structures" (pp. 7,9).

In the conclusion to the NCATE Report (2000), it was noted there exists a "preponderance of evidence of a high level collaboration by all stakeholders," recognizing the partnership's "serious and sustained attention to learning" (p. 18). Further, the network was commended "as a lever for change in the educational reform movement at both the school and university level and as a model for PDS development in the larger professional community locally, regionally, and nationally" (NCATE, 2000, p. 19).

The network's development was further influenced by the NCATE PDS Standards as Maryland developed its own PDS standards. Recognizing that no mechanism existed to determine whether PDS partnerships met the intent of the *Redesign of Teacher Education*, the Maryland Partnership for Teaching and Learning K–16 convened the Superintendents and Deans Committee to create PDS standards and developmental guidelines for Maryland PDS partnerships. The members of the Superintendents and Deans Committee drafted standards and indicators to reflect the NCATE PDS standards, address the *Redesign*, and to create guidelines designed to shape implementation and help determine the developmental level of Maryland PDS efforts.

Faculty from Towson University and its P–12 PDS schools were active participants in this multi-year process, working with representatives of the Superintendents and Deans Committee to ensure that the standards reflected the real world of P–12 schools and the university. Once the initial standards were drafted, statewide PDS practitioners convened for a three-day Leadership Academy focused on helping P–16 PDS faculty prepare for a site visit and training PDS site visitors. For this Leadership Academy, Towson University and Owings Mills Elementary School faculty shared the materials they had developed for the NCATE PDS Standards Project and created a virtual PDS visit including mock interviews.

Having served as a pilot site for the NCATE Standards Project, Towson volunteered to field test the *Standards for Maryland Professional Development Schools*. A Towson University-Howard County Public Schools elementary PDS engaged university personnel, two principals, a boundary-spanning instructional facilitator, a central office representative, and two school faculties in an extensive, year-long self-study culminating in a highly successful, multi-day, on-site visit by a P–16 state team. Input from this pilot effort (and that at three other host sites) resulted in further revision of Maryland's PDS standards.

The purpose of the site visits was to test the PDS standards and developmental guidelines and make recommendations for changes. In addition to participating in one of the site visits, other university faculty served as members of visiting teams to other PDS sites engaged in the pilot process. Input from this pilot (and three other host sites) resulted in the final revision of Maryland's PDS Standards and Developmental Guidelines. These frameworks provide guidance for all Maryland higher education institutions and local school systems in the development and sustaining of PDS. The standards now serve as the basis for site visits to PDS as part of Maryland's program approval and accreditation process.

Several Towson-related studies (previously cited) have resulted in reports confirming the positive impact of the network. Equally important, network priorities have been validated by numerous external evaluations. In turn, providing sustained professional development for in-service teachers has been and continues to be a distinguishing characteristic of the Towson PDS Network. An external evaluation of Maryland PDS conducted in 1997 by The Mid-Atlantic Laboratory for Student Success at Temple University concluded that the numerous growth opportunities that characterized the network positively impacted practicing teachers' teaching styles since practitioners had more access to research and were more aware of their own teaching styles because they were mentoring future teachers.

Based on its review of the PDS network, the Association of Teacher Educators granted its 1998 Distinguished Teacher Education award to Towson having determined

> the PDS network with Towson University is a model for a true collaborative partnership. University personnel understand that a PDS is more than a location for placing student teachers. The Towson model looks at what the university can do to support professional development of in-service teachers and to impact student achievement. It benefits the school system and is what the system will expect of all of its higher education partners. (p. 7)

Finally, in his third assessment (1995–1996, 1997–1998, 2000–2001) of the degree Maryland's higher education institutions have implemented the *Redesign*, former Deputy Secretary of the Maryland Higher Education Commission, George Funaro concluded, "Towson University displays a pervasive commitment to the tenets of the *Redesign*," had "totally embraced the [PDS] concept" and as a result was "offering students a research-based, cutting-edge teacher preparation program" (2002, p. 39).

Institutionalization: PDS as Foundation

Fully committed to PDS and seeking to further institutionalize its culture of P–16 collaboration, Towson has developed and implemented several new initiatives. First, expectations and responsibilities for new Towson University faculty have evolved to include addressing the needs of pre-service and in-service teachers specifically through PDS site-based course delivery and the integration of teacher education with school improvement plans.

Second, concurrent with its PDS goals and in conjunction with school systems' professional development offices, Towson has offered multiple graduate courses for partners at PDS sites. Ensuing discussions formalized the structure for continuing professional development opportunities for in-service teachers that became known as the Towson Learning Network (TLN). The collaborative and entrepreneurial nature of TLN reduced out-of-pocket expenses for in-service teachers taking courses, significantly increased graduate enrollments and credit hours produced, and provided revenue redistribution to College of Education units involved in course delivery that serve as a continuous revenue stream to institutionalize PDS.

Third, in July 2001, pursuing its vision to serve as a national leader in promoting inquiry about and documenting the impact of PDS, Towson created its Institute for Professional Development School Studies. The main goal is to examine the impacts of PDS activity on P–12 students, in-service teachers, university interns and faculty, as well as parents and communities. Its initial study, a longitudinal study of the impact of PDS preparation on attrition/retention and student achievement, was begun in Summer 2002.

Conclusion

"A Community of Learners," the theme of the Towson Professional Development School Network, has been the driving force behind network implementation. The network has been successful because it has been a systemic effort, a P–16 collaboration linking the best of practice with the best of theory and research, thus preparing and sustaining the abilities of teachers to teach well and have a positive impact on student achievement. The network promotes fundamental change not by prescription but through challenging involvement and problem solving for all stakeholders, by allowing structures to emerge in ways that support change instead of constraining change within existing cultures, by dignifying the knowledge teachers possess, and by offering leadership and professional growth opportunities to university and school faculty. The network is as much about the reculturing of schools and professional development as about the restructuring of schools and professional development; thereby, making individual PDS partnerships and the network into places in which a culture of professional development is stimulated and supported.

Much has been accomplished and learned by the network partners as they enter a ninth year of existence. Their experiences continue to inform the growth and development of the network. The extended and intensive internship continues to provide interns the rich opportunity to be immersed in the realities of school culture and become members of the community of learners. Numerous professional development opportunities continue to be designed and delivered collaboratively in a variety of formats to meet the varying needs of practicing or in-service teachers and university faculty. University faculty have broadened and modified their practices as a result of their sustained involvement in public schools. The central focus remains the same: improved student learning.

While expanding the network and celebrating success, Towson also recognizes that ongoing challenges remain. Changes in P–16 leadership at the state and local levels, the need for ongoing as well as entrepreneurial funding mechanisms, demands for accountability, issues of sustainability, and the need for faculty expansion continue to pose challenges to the Towson PDS Network.

Note

1. In recognition and support of its Professional Development School Network, Towson University has received approximately $1,900,000 in PDS grants.

References

Abdal-Haqq, I. (1995). *PDS: A directory of projects in the U.S.* Washington, DC: AACTE Clinical Schools Clearinghouse.

Abdal-Haqq, I. (1998). *Professional development schools: Weighing the evidence.* Thousand Oaks, CA: Corwin Press.

Altwerger, B. & Cole, L. (1997). *The Owings Mills Elementary–Towson University PDS evaluation report.* Unpublished report. Towson University, Towson, MD.

Association of Teacher Educators Newsletter (1998). *A network of professional development schools.* May-June 1998. pp. 5–7.

Berry, B., & Catoe, S. (1994). Creating professional development schools. In L. Darling-Hammond (Ed.), *Professional development schools: Schools for developing a profession* (pp. 176–202). New York: Teachers College Press.

Book, C. (1996). Professional development schools. In J. Sikula, T. Buttery, & E. Guyton (Eds.), *Handbook of research on teacher education* (2nd ed., pp. 194–212). New York: Simon and Schuster Macmillan.

Carnegie Forum. (1986). *A nation prepared: Teachers for the twenty-first century.* New York: Carnegie Forum on Education and the Economy.

Clark, R. W. (1999). *Effective professional development schools: Agenda for education in a democracy.* Vol. 3. San Francisco: Jossey-Bass Publishers.

Cuban, L. (1988). *The managerial imperative and the practice of leadership in schools.* Albany: State University of New York Press.

Darling-Hammond, L. (Ed.) (1994). *Professional development schools: Schools for developing a profession.* New York: Teachers College Press.

Field, T, & Barksdale-Ladd, M. (1994). A changing school. In Reed, W. (Ed), *Lessons from experiences in school restructuring.* Albany: SUNY Press.

Funaro, G. (2002). *Final report: Teacher preparation programs and the Redesign of Teacher Education.* Baltimore: Maryland Higher Education Commission and the Maryland State Department of Education.

Hinkle, D, & Proffitt, T. (1996). The community of learning: A laboratory for the professional development of educators. In *Building the institutional capacity in support of education preparation within the context of shared responsibility.* Renaissance Group Proceedings, November 1996.

Holmes Group. (1986). *Tomorrow's teachers: A report of The Holmes Group.* East Lansing, MI: The Holmes Group.

Holmes Group. (1990). *Tomorrow's schools: Principles for the design of professional development schools.* East Lansing, MI: The Holmes Group.

Holmes Group. (1995). *Tomorrow's schools of education: A report of the Holmes Group*. East Lansing, MI: The Holmes Group.

Laboratory for Student Success, the Mid-Atlantic Regional Educational Laboratory. (1997). *Maryland consortium of professional development schools: An evaluation of implementation and outcomes*. Philadelphia: Temple University.

Levine, M. (Ed.). (1988). *Professional practice schools: Building a model*. Washington, DC: American Federation of Teachers.

Maryland Higher Education Commission. (1995). *Teacher education task force report: Redesign of teacher education*. Annapolis, MD: Author.

Maryland Partnership for Teaching and Learning K-16, Superintendents and Deans Committee. (2001). *Professional development schools: An implementation manual*. Baltimore: Author.

Maryland State Department of Education. (1998a). *Maryland partnership for teaching and learning K-16*. Baltimore, MD: Author.

Maryland State Department of Education. (1998b). *A review of professional development schools in Maryland: State teacher education council, 1995–1997 report*. Baltimore, MD: Author.

Maryland State Department of Education. (1998c). *Towson University Report*. Baltimore, MD: Author.

Maxwell, D., Morgan, P., & Proffitt, T. (1999). *Towson University – Baltimore County Public Schools PDS network: Internal evaluation report*. Unpublished report. Towson University, Towson, MD.

National Alliance of Business. (2001). *Investing in teaching*. New York: Author.

National Commission on Excellence in Education. (1983). *A nation at risk: The imperative for education reform*. Washington, DC: U.S. Department of Education.

National Commission on Teaching and America's Future. (1996). *Doing what matters most: Investing in quality teaching*. New York: Author.

National Council for the Accreditation of Teacher Education. (2000). *Site visit report, NCATE PDS Draft Standards Pilot Project: Towson University/Owings Mills Elementary School PDS Partnership*. Washington, DC: Author.

Neubert, G., & Binko, J. (1998). Professional development schools—The proof is in the performance. *Educational Leadership*, February 1998, pp. 44–46.

Proffitt, T., Field, T., Hinkle, D., & Pilato, V. (1996). Commissioned Paper: *Expanding individual P–12/HE partnerships to networks*. Renaissance Group Conference, Baltimore, MD, October 1996.

Richmond, D. (1998). *Effect of involvement in a PDS on certified teachers*. Unpublished master's thesis, Towson University, Towson, MD.

Teitel, L. (1998). Professional development schools: A literature review. In Marsha Levine (Ed.), *Designing standards that work for professional development schools* (33–80). Washington, DC: NCATE.

Teitel, L. (2001a). An assessment framework for professional development schools: Going beyond the leap of faith. *Journal of Teacher Education*, January/February, 2001, 57–69.

Teitel, L. (2001b). *How professional development schools make a difference: A review of research*. Washington, DC: NCATE.

Yarrison, B. (1996). *Impact of teacher training programs on perceptions of preparedness of first year teachers*. Unpublished master's thesis, Towson University, Towson, MD.

PART TWO

Gaining Entrée to School Districts and Schools

CHAPTER TWO

Becoming Teachers: The First Professional Development School Partnership in Maryland

Lynn C. Cole, Bess Altwerger,
Lisa Joy Greenberg, & Jessica Wolf Rhoten

The way I sum up my experiences is that we are becoming teachers...instead of learning how to be teachers.

Jessica Wolf Rhoten

A Look at the First Professional Development School Partnership in Maryland

In Room 204, students sling their book bags and lunches in the coat closet, talk to each other about their weekend, and finally settle down to listen to morning announcements. Everyone stands for the pledge of allegiance to the flag with a greater understanding of symbolism and abstractions like liberty, justice, and democracy that they have been exploring in their social studies projects. Their personal reflections on these concepts are expressed in poems that fill the bulletin board by the flag. After the pledge, the students and their teacher grab copies of *Number the Stars, Roll of Thunder, Hear My Cry*, and *My Brother Sam Is Dead*, books that also have themes of freedom, loyalty, and allegiance. Some students dive for carpet squares while others remain in their seats hunched over, legs stretched out, or sitting sideways in desks too small for their bodies this early in the morning. The rocker, a place of privilege, is reserved for the teacher during Read Aloud time. Today after DEAR time, they will discuss *Number the Stars* in Literature Circles. Jessica, Tammy, and Kelly will be asked to wear yellow stars pinned to their sleeves. The three students talk about how the stars, just symbols, make them feel uncomfortable, even in the tight, safe circle on the floor. The teacher discovers that most of the students do not know why Sweden was a safe harbor for the

Jews in the story. The class knows geography will be an upcoming mini-lesson, especially since they also could not locate Bosnia during Vicki's current events presentation yesterday. The teacher has brought in pink cupcakes to celebrate the conclusion of the book and has announced she has planned a field trip to the Holocaust Museum in Washington, DC. After the Literature Circle, the teacher reviews the schedule for the day written on a chalkboard at the front of the room:

❑   Conduct running records on children you are assessing for the Literacy Evaluation and Instruction Portfolios
❑   Participate in Demonstration Improvement Work in inquiry study groups on the Integrated Theme Study for social studies and reading class
❑   Mrs. Greenberg on Graphic Organizers
❑   Present Social Action Project plans to the School Team after school

The teacher explains that when Mrs. Greenberg, in the room across the hall, can leave her class with the instructional assistant, she will come in to discuss how she uses graphic organizers and semantic webs with her second graders. Then, the teacher resumes her circulating and has individual conferences with students.

This could be any fifth grade classroom, but instead, it is a classroom of university interns who are elementary education juniors at the University. All of their professional classes are "delivered" in this unique "university" classroom where they experience the strategies and practices they will be encouraged to use with the elementary students at this same school.

Reflection Through the Eyes of an Intern (Jessica)

As I sat cross-legged on the oversized carpet with the rest of my classmates, I looked up at my professor with feelings of excitement and anticipation growing inside me. She had just called all of her students back to the carpet to sit around the rocking chair for a read-aloud.

"Why do you think slaves were not permitted to learn to read and write?" she asked us. Several students shared their predictions before the teacher said, "We'll find out if your ideas were on track after we hear the story, *Sweet Clara and the Freedom Quilt*."

As the story was read aloud to us, I remember experiencing a wave of emotions. First, I felt sheer delight; here I was, twenty years old, being read to aloud from a children's picture book. It felt so wonderful! I truly enjoyed hearing my teacher's expression and interpretation of the story. I recall thinking to myself, *This is how I want my future students—no matter what age they may be—to feel when I read aloud to them.* At the same time, I was feeling a sense of loss and found myself wondering, *Why do teachers stop reading aloud to their students after their students are able to read on their own?* It was at this moment that I made a mental note always to read aloud to students as part of their reading instruction—no matter how old or competent they were at reading. Finally, the story itself evoked several emotions; mainly, I felt pride in Sarah's cleverness and ability to overcome her own obstacles.

After the story was discussed and predictions to the teacher's original question were revisited, it was apparent I was not the only student to experience such a wave of emotion. The consensus of the group was this had been a positive and effective approach to teaching reading. Having reflected on our teacher's modeling of the read-aloud strategy, we were expected to choose a children's picture book to share with a classroom of elementary students later in the week.

The climate in which our reading methods course instruction took place contributed greatly to the success of the read-aloud. Had my university professor and my classmates been in a traditional university campus classroom in contrast to a public elementary school classroom for the modeling of this instructional approach, we would not have been as engaged and the experience would not have been as authentic. The experience was intensified because we were reminded of what our future students could experience under our instruction in the same setting—a caring teacher, carpet squares, and a rocking chair. I cannot help but wonder, *Shouldn't all pre-service teachers have such positive and personally engaging learning experiences?*

Reflection Through the Eyes of a Classroom Teacher (Lisa)

I ventured across the hallway to the university classroom where I could be reflective about my own teaching. The university professors had asked me to demonstrate how I used graphic organizers with my second graders. I was so excited about sharing a "real" perspective with interns. I remember being energized in this learning environment and felt fortunate to be part of such an exciting paradigm shift in teacher education. Imagine being a university intern and hearing about a particular teaching style or technique, and, then, being able to walk down the hallway to observe it! This must have been quite a powerful learning experience, and I kept thinking and I wished I could have had the same opportunity. I knew the university interns would walk away more prepared to teach and so, too, would all of the stakeholders benefit in many ways: children and their parents, classroom teachers, and principals.

These personal reflections begin to tell the story of Maryland's first professional development school partnership between Towson University and the Baltimore County Public Schools. In the rest of this chapter, the characteristics of this PDS and the research conducted about the first interns who graduated will be described. Data were collected throughout the PDS program and during the first year of teaching of these interns. The findings confirmed the benefits of such a radical departure from traditional teacher education programs, and provided the impetus for expanding the implementation of professional development school partnerships across Maryland. The success of this first professional development school partnership also encouraged experimentation with other innovative program designs.

Description of the Professional Development School Partnership

In Spring 1994, the principal of Owings Mills Elementary School obtained permission from the county to re-employ his existing faculty and employ new faculty who desired to be a part of the a professional development school. The faculty and school administration participated in summer course work and summer strategic planning conducted by the university faculty in preparation for the beginning of this "new school." In Fall 1994, the first cohort of junior Elementary Education majors, interns, were randomly selected to participate in this new teacher education program.

The school was to be the interns' "campus" for course work and field experiences throughout the last two years of the undergraduate program. This contrasted significantly with the traditional program in which students were placed at different school sites within different school systems each semester for field experiences while being on campus for coursework. Although student teaching historically had taken place in "center-schools" to which groups of students were assigned, this program was the first to extend residency in a single school site for the entire professional program. The student body at the school was diverse with regard to cultural and ethnic background, learning needs, and academic performance. This along with zero-based staffing made this a viable single-site model where interns gained intimate knowledge of the daily workings of a public school. They formed strong relationships with students, faculty, and parents, and became a part of the larger school community as teachers who would remain in one school for a year or more.

Because the field-based assignments and course work took place during all-day blocks of time in classrooms at the school, there was a much greater opportunity for using "class times" creatively by scheduling classroom visitations of varying durations and optimizing opportunities for students to examine relationships between theoretical and pedagogical concepts and classroom practices. This "on-site residency" was a significant contrast to the traditional program with a rigid half-day or one day per week schedule. Field experiences ranged from an hour to a number of consecutive days depending upon the goals and purposes of assignments. Rather than being restricted to one classroom for a field experience during a traditional semester, field placements for the PDS interns in the Elementary Education program spanned grades K–5, providing opportunities to examine broader developmental and curricular issues.

A classroom to call "their own" was essential to creating a learning environment for interns where the establishment and maintenance of a classroom and instructional methodologies and practices associated with excellence in teaching could be modeled, not just described. For example, a classroom library of children's literature books was used to model independent reading, literature study, individual conferencing, shared reading, and small group guided reading. Writing materials, a writing center, and a classroom computer were part of a writing workshop program in which interns used all of the steps in the writing process to produce their own writing portfolios. Interns learned pedagogical practices through actual experience, rather than only through readings and presentations. These same instructional strategies could be practiced by interns with students in the school. Interns assumed responsibilities typical of practicing teachers, such as creating a classroom library, using learning centers, designing bulletin boards, planning meeting spaces, and finding and retrieving instructional resources. This classroom in the school was where interns could bring students for instruction, meet with visitors, and watch classroom teachers demonstrate strategies.

Two university professors accepted responsibility for developing, teaching, and coordinating the teacher education curriculum. Except for a semester focused on mathematics and the sciences, the professors co-planned and team-taught all of the professional courses and supervised the field assignments. The courses included Reading/Language Arts, Social Studies, and Foundations of Education. This arrangement provided opportunities to deliver a more coordinated, consistent professional preparation program. A consistent philosophical and theoretical perspective was maintained throughout the program and could be modeled through instructional strategies and class assignments. Opportunities for comparison and contrast arose through professional readings and multiple field-based observations outside of the professional development school.

Each semester interns were provided with a consolidated and integrated syllabus rather than several separate syllabi. The consolidated syllabus provided a plan for organized course content around a single set of learning goals. Assignments and projects were coordinated and integrated, providing interns with a more efficient and cohesive set of expectations. For example, assignments for Social Studies, Reading, Language Arts, and Children's Literature could be coordinated and integrated through comprehensive research projects and instructional plans about various historical events, social issues, or cultural studies. Field-based classroom assignments were coordinated to accomplish a set of cohesive curricular goals. Consistent and coordinated instruction over a two-year time period allowed for long-term spiraling of the curriculum through revisiting, expanding, and refining concepts and skills throughout the professional program.

Knowing Is Not Enough

Everyone involved in creating the PDS knew it was a worthwhile endeavor despite the labor intensity accompanying such an effort. The interns knew they were a part of something new, exciting, and more challenging. The classroom teachers knew the PDS experience was more intensive and more real-life than their own teacher education training. They knew they were helping to shape future colleagues who would begin teaching with the strengths and skills of second-year teachers. University faculty knew their teaching would never be the same. They realized that teaching interns *about teaching* could never replace showing interns how to *become teachers*. But, could it be proven that this was a better way of educating university interns?

Research Goals

In order to ascertain the effectiveness of the PDS model, data were collected at three different points during the two-year teacher education program and during the students' first year of teaching following graduation. There was a control group of randomly selected students from the various other cohorts in the traditional program.

For the research conducted during the teacher education program, the focus was on:

- Knowledge, awareness, and sensitivity to issues of cultural diversity and the level of experience, competence, and confidence in teaching culturally diverse student populations
- Level of professional development and socialization to the teaching profession
- Attainment of content knowledge, including theoretical concepts and pedagogical practice
- Knowledge of and experience with using technology to support instructional goals of the classroom
- Perceived level of preparedness for and confidence in obtaining a teaching position following graduation.

For the research conducted during the first year of teaching, the focus was on the effect of the PDS experience on novice teachers:

- Preparedness for and acclimation to beginning teaching
- Success in the role of first-year teacher
- Implementation of a reading/language arts curriculum framed in a clear theoretical orientation and responsive to the diversity of student needs
- Satisfaction with their chosen profession.

Method

During the two-year professional program, data from the PDS cohort and control groups were obtained through questionnaires and videotaped interviews. Questionnaires consisted of Likert-scale items and responses to short answer questions directly related to the areas of investigation. Data were analyzed using descriptive statistics. Written responses were analyzed in order to support and extend quantitative findings. Data from the Elementary Education program evaluation questionnaire distributed to all students completing the student teaching internship were analyzed to determine the effects of the PDS on student perceptions of competence and confidence in teaching. Videotaped interviews were conducted with the PDS cohort and the control group separately and, then, as an integrated group. Interviews were conducted by university faculty who were not directly involved in the instructional program. The interviews were analyzed for topic and theme of discussion, differences and similarities between groups, and to corroborate and extend quantitative findings.

During the first year of teaching, graduates of the professional development school program (who obtained teaching positions in the Baltimore-Washington area) were visited by a member of the evaluation team three times: September-October, February-March, and early June. These teachers completed a Likert-scale and short-answer questionnaire, and they were interviewed using a standard protocol. Using observation checklists, data were also collected on various aspects of the classroom environment and teacher interactions with students. During each of the three school visits, an interview was conducted with the principal or other supervisory personnel (such as teacher-mentors) who were asked to complete a brief Likert-scale questionnaire. During the second and third rounds of data collection, questionnaires identical to those completed by the first-year teacher graduates of the PDS were sent to all Elementary Education graduates of the traditional program in order to establish a basis for comparing program effects.

Data Analysis: PDS Interns and the Control Groups

Due to the small sample of students involved in the evaluation, statistical significance was not established. However, programmatic significance could be determined by noting consistent discrepancies between the PDS group and the control groups in the areas of knowledge, awareness, and sensitivity to issues of cultural diversity and the level of experience, competence, and confidence in teaching culturally diverse student populations.

A goal of the faculty in the university's Department of Elementary Education was to produce teachers who exhibited positive attitudes toward diversity and who were competent to teach in a wide range of school settings. Diversity was seriously considered in adopting the PDS site, developing the instructional program, and planning the evaluation agenda. The demographics of the student population at the PDS, located in a suburban setting, were comparable to those of more urban settings. Additionally, students with disabilities were included in most of the classrooms.

The instructional program developed for the interns at the PDS placed great emphasis on developing a knowledge and awareness of cultural diversity and gaining experience in teaching a wide range of students. Projects, assignments, guest speakers, and field trips were reflective of this instructional goal. The traditional campus-based program also emphasized diversity as a goal for professional development. However, in contrast to the PDS, students in the traditional program were assigned to school sites in two or three different school systems, including a city school during the first semester of the program. Would it be possible, then, for the interns in the PDS to develop the requisite knowledge and attitudes about teaching in diverse settings even with a strong programmatic emphasis on diversity? Through an analysis of data, the following conclusions were reached.

1. **Despite a single school suburban placement, interns in the PDS rated themselves very high in awareness and experience with diverse student populations.**

Consistently, all questionnaire and interview data indicated that interns in the PDS partnership considered themselves to be highly aware of cultural diversity and highly experienced with teaching diverse populations. By the end of the program they rated themselves an average of 2.98 out of a possible 3.0 on knowledge of and experience with diversity. On the standard Elementary Education evaluation form distributed to all teacher candidates, PDS interns rated themselves very highly (an average of 1.2 with 1.0 as the highest on a 1–5 scale) on multicultural awareness and experience. This was consistent with students in multiple field placements across different school systems.

2. **All interns in the PDS who intended to teach indicated a strong likelihood they would apply to an urban school system. None of the control group responded in this manner.**

The interns in the professional development school partnership were not assigned to a city school during their first semester in the professional sequence as were students in the traditional program. During their student teaching semester, the students in the traditional program spent one week visiting a city school and one week in a suburban or rural school of their choosing. At the conclusion of the program, the interns, unlike their traditional counterparts in the control group, rated themselves as likely or very likely to apply to an urban school system. From interview data, it was indicated the interns felt competent and confident to teach in a wide range of settings, including those in urban environments.

3. Interns in the PDS reported greater knowledge and experience with the school community, organization and routines of schools and classrooms, and greater collegiality with school faculty and administration.

It was consistently indicated that intensive and extensive field experiences at the PDS provided interns with a clear and realistic sense of school and classroom organization. Over the course of the program, they cited an ever-increasing familiarity and comfort with school culture and the role of teachers in the school community. One student said,

> The very first thing I remember is the faculty meeting. I just felt like I was starting with everybody at the same time. I wasn't coming in as a stranger. I feel even now that I can go up to anyone in the school and ask them a question and get help from them without feeling bad or feeling it was some trouble for them.

4. Interns in the professional development school partnership indicated commitment to PDS school students and faculty as the key motivator for their professional studies and pedagogical improvement.

A continual theme found in the interview data and written responses was the interns' strong sense of commitment to the students and faculty at the PDS. The following example, taken from interview after only the first year of residency at the school illustrates this sense of commitment,

> I think a lot is because it matters now. It is not just a college course that you are taking. We are at the PDS site. We are a part of that school and those kids mean something to us. We have already developed a bond with those kids. They come to us and they have things they want to share with us...like what happened to them over the weekend at home. You feel like you owe them something back. So, the work that we put into this...has to be top notch. Because, that's what you want to give to the kids. That's what you want to give back to them.

This statement is representative of a generalized shift in the perspective of the interns from that of university students to becoming developing professionals. Interviews with the control group at the beginning of the program were focused around topics such as course workload and assignments, grading, and sequencing of courses. Some control group students mentioned a feeling of alienation and discomfort in their field sites. It is important to note that traditional students spent only one half day a week in the first semester and one full day a week in the second semester in their field placement schools. Due to the residency of the professional program at the PDS site, interns spent part of each instructional day in the school building.

5. **Interns in the PDS indicated they developed strong collegial bonds and a sense of belonging to the school community.**

Interns in the PDS consistently cited their collegial relationships with school personnel as among the most beneficial aspects of their program. They reported an ease of interaction and sense of camaraderie rarely cited by the students in the traditional program prior to the student teaching semester. Interns reported feeling comfortable approaching a large number of staff members for support and assistance. A student said,

> I think my peak experience was when I was teaching full time, just the closeness that I felt with the teachers, not just the fifth grade teachers, but the whole team. We had lunch together every day. We discussed that I was having this problem and they would say, "Well, I would do this." I felt like I was one of the teachers. I was on a personal level. It wasn't, "you are a student and I am a teacher." It was more like, "we are partners and we will help each other out." It was so great. Immediate feedback all the time. Every five minutes it would be like "that was great. Why don't you try this now?" It wasn't two days after my lesson of three weeks after my lesson. It was DURING my lesson. I had a write-up afterwards. I knew exactly what I was doing all the time.

Interns in the PDS consistently expressed a feeling of belonging to the school as a welcomed and accepted member of the school community. By the end of the third semester of the program, just prior to the student teaching semester, the interns rated themselves higher on questionnaire items pertaining to acclimation and socialization to teaching (4.6 on a scale to 5, with 5.0 as the highest possible rating, as opposed to 3.4 for the control group). Thus, immersion at the PDS was valuable.

6. **Interns in the PDS indicated a high level of awareness regarding the range of instructional and management strategies and a highly developed sense of what characteristics constitute good instruction.**

In contrast to the traditional practice of placing a student with one teacher for each of the field experiences, interns were assigned to a range of classrooms and grade levels throughout the two years at the PDS. They reported a high level of awareness of the range of instructional and management strategies available to teachers. Interviews and written responses from these interns indicated a greater sense of confidence regarding their ability to manage instruction and behavior prior to the student teaching experience. They cited purposeful, active, multicultural instruction as necessary in accommodating the diverse strengths and needs of students. They reported having a clear vision of best practices for which they could strive during the course of their professional development. They credited their extensive experiences in classrooms (as well as the modeling of best practices in their on-site university courses) as contributing to this vision:

> In our classroom, I found it was really interesting to learn by doing. There were so many things we didn't know we were learning. Maybe another cohort had it actually listed down in sentence format [in a syllabus]. We didn't realize we were even learning it because we were actually doing it in the classroom. Reading books, sharing book talks...all of that, we actually did just like a classroom in elementary school.

7. **Interns in the PDS rated their pedagogical knowledge as highly as their control group counterparts did in the traditional program and higher in math and science content knowledge.**

There was no discernable difference between the interns in the PDS and control groups in their ratings of pedagogical knowledge in most areas. Both groups reflected confidence in their basic knowledge of pedagogical content. However after the third semester of the program, which included math and science course work taught at the PDS site, it was indicated that PDS interns had greater confidence than the control group in their knowledge of these content areas.

To determine whether the students' knowledge base was equal to or higher than that of the control group, the results of the National Teachers Exam were analyzed. Comparing the mean scores of the interns in the PDS vs. the general Elementary Education group of students, it was found that the PDS interns achieved higher mean scores on the Professional Knowledge and Elementary Education Specialty subtests of the National Teachers Exam than did their counterparts in the traditional program.

8. Interns found that their knowledge of and experience with using technology supported instructional goals of the classroom.

Interns in the PDS received a three-credit, rather than the traditional one-credit, course in instructional technology. Assignments and course content for the instructional technology course were integrated and coordinated with the content and classroom field assignments of the other professional courses.

Interviews with the interns revealed high regard for the integrated nature of their technology course work. They commented on the advantages of assignments that were relevant and supportive to their classroom teaching and other professional studies. In contrast, interviews with the control group interns indicated that though they found their one-credit instructional technology course beneficial, they viewed it as insufficient and unrelated to the rest of their professional course work and field experiences.

9. Interns in the PDS and their peers agreed that technology (especially electronic communication) should be a higher priority in the professional program and selection of field sites.

From interviews, the students indicated that experiences with using instructional technology varied greatly across school and classroom placements during student teaching. Interns reiterated their praise for the three-credit instructional technology course in the first year of their program, but they indicated disappointment in the level at which instructional technology was integrated with classroom instruction at the PDS site. Although this varied from classroom to classroom, computer use at that time was generally confined to the pull-out technology program in the computer lab. Interns agreed with their control group peers that the professional program should have an even-greater emphasis on instructional technology and electronic communication in particular. They suggested that technologically advanced schools be recruited for field placements during the professional program.

10. Interns perceived a high level of preparedness for and confidence in obtaining a teaching position following graduation.

One of the goals of a teacher education program is to graduate teacher candidates who feel confident in their preparedness for their first year of teaching and confident in their ability to present themselves positively during the interview process. Questionnaire and interview items were selected to determine the extent of this concern.

It was indicated that those interns intending to teach in the following school year had strong confidence in obtaining a teaching position. The interns anticipated (and in some cases had experienced) successful interviews with school personnel. One comment made during the videotaped group discussion indicated there would be "little a principal or recruiter could ask that she would be unable to answer."

11. Interns in the PDS indicated a high level of confidence in succeeding in a wide range of school settings.

Regardless of the single school residency, the interns expressed their confidence that they could teach in a variety of school settings and with a wide range of students. Overall findings in this area suggested that early and sustained immersion in schools provided students with the positive attitude they needed in seeking and obtaining teaching positions.

Data Analysis: Graduates' First Year of Teaching

An important goal of a professional program is to produce teachers who are competent and confident in their ability to assume the full responsibility of teaching. Though it would seem reasonable to predict that first-year teachers who had been immersed in school communities for two years would acclimate more easily to the role of teacher and public school life, it was necessary to determine if this were actually the case. A research goal set for the initial round of data collection focused on obtaining the requisite information.

1. The interns were prepared for and acclimatized to beginning teaching.

Triangulated data derived from questionnaires and interviews with the teachers and principals and focused classroom observations revealed that the graduates were:

- Competent and confident in assuming the responsibilities of teaching.
- Prepared with a repertoire of strategies to organize and manage the learning environment.
- Prepared for the workload and demands of the teaching profession.
- Adjusting well to becoming members of their faculties and school communities.
- Prepared to interact with and teach culturally diverse student populations.
- Prepared to use technology to support their classroom instruction.

Interestingly, the principals of schools where these graduates were employed rated the former interns higher than the former interns rated themselves in all but one of these areas. This implies that first-year teachers who graduated from the PDS maintained extremely high standards for their own performance. However in the area of technology, these same teachers rated themselves higher than their principals did in preparedness to use technology to enhance learning in their classrooms (teachers = 3.0; principals = 2.4, on a 1–4 scale, with 4 as the highest score). As the interns suggested, this indicates that the selection of more technologically advanced school sites for pre-service field experiences is important.

Observations made at the beginning of the school year supported the findings described above. Furthermore, observations of the teachers who were former interns indicated they had successfully established classroom routines and an organized classroom environment, effective classroom management, and clearly stated learning goals and objectives. In the interviews, it was also noted that at this early point in the school year, the former interns had not experienced disappointment in choosing teaching as their career a felt successful in their initial teaching. Principals revealed they viewed the teachers as unusually well prepared and successful as beginning teachers.

The new teachers, former PDS interns, identified the following as the most beneficial features of their professional program in preparing them for a smooth transition to the world of teaching:

- The intensive and extensive nature of their field experiences.
- On-site residency of the professional program.
- Intact peer cohort throughout the two-year program.

The interview data indicated that interns in the PDS considered their extended and intensive experiences in schools and classrooms as extremely beneficial to their professional growth and development. They attributed their comfort in the school community and their sense of belonging and commitment to the students and faculty at the PDS to the on-site residency of the professional program, especially the dedicated classroom. Throughout their program and continuing into their first year of teaching, the interns confirmed the importance of their professional relationships with their cohort peers about professional growth and development. In their comments they indicated the support network which developed from their two-year association had continued into their first year of teaching and that this had motivated them to establish collegial support within their new school faculties.

In the second and third rounds of data collection at mid-year and end-of-year during the first year of teaching of the graduates, the following were also added as a focus:

- Success in the role of first-year teacher.
- Implementation of a reading/language arts curriculum framed in a clear theoretical orientation and responsive to the diversity of student needs.
- Satisfaction with their chosen profession.

All of the teachers who had been PDS interns reported they had been successful in their roles as first-year teachers. Their ratings for success in the teaching profession were maintained or increased throughout this first year. They reported a sense of competence and confidence in assuming the responsibilities of teaching. They reported they believed they had attained a knowledge of curriculum content sufficient to implement an effective instructional program. They were able to create a rich classroom literacy environment reflective of the cultural identity of their students. They also rated themselves highly in implementing instructional strategies to meet the varying academic needs of their students. The former interns' ratings for preparedness for the workload and demands of teaching were maintained or increased throughout their first year of teaching. It was interesting to note that teachers who had been PDS interns rated their competence and confidence in teaching and their preparedness with instructional strategies higher than did other teacher education graduates who had obtained teaching positions.

The principals continued to rate teachers who were former PDS interns highly in their preparedness for and success during the first year of teaching. All of the principals agreed that the former interns were well suited for the teaching profession, especially in the implementation of a reading/language arts curriculum framed in a clear theoretical orientation and responsive to the diversity of student needs.

Given the strong emphasis on language arts instructional strategies in the undergraduate program, data were collected to determine whether PDS teacher graduates experienced success in teaching this curriculum area. Also, there was interest in assessing whether or not former PDS interns would maintain their stated philosophical stance toward reading and language arts instruction throughout the school year and ascertaining whether or not their philosophical stance was reflected in their classroom practice.

2. **All teacher graduates from the PDS maintained a clearly stated philosophy of reading and language arts instruction throughout the year.**

Teachers who were former PDS interns reported that throughout their first year of teaching they used the wide range of reading and language arts strategies they learned in the professional program. Observations confirmed these reports. The former interns reported their philosophical positions remained largely unchanged, except for increased awareness of the range of student ability. Their philosophy statements written during each data collection period reflected an orientation towards literature-based, meaning-driven, integrated language arts instruction. However, some of these teachers expressed concerns about imposed language arts programs and assessments, lack of adequate reading materials, demands of record keeping and paperwork. The principals confirmed their overall satisfaction with the reading and language arts programs implemented in the classrooms of these teachers.

Throughout the first year of teaching, the teachers who were graduates of the PDS remained satisfied with teaching as their chosen profession. They became increasingly convinced that teaching was the best career choice for them and expected to remain in the teaching profession. None of these teachers expected to pursue non-teaching career options. All expected to have an advanced degree in education within the next 10 years. However, two areas of concern were consistently reported throughout the school year.

The first concern involved the perceived inadequacy of resources and materials to create learning environments they had envisioned. It is interesting to note the principals did not concur. They indicated that the teachers were provided with adequate resources and materials. However, classroom observations supported teacher reports. A discrepancy was noted in the quantity and quality of resources provided to teacher-graduates of the PDS, especially in terms of reading materials, technology, and curriculum content materials. Teachers who graduated from the PDS rated the adequacy of resources lower than other teacher-graduates who had obtained teaching positions.

The second concern involved perceived limitations on the opportunity for the teacher-graduates to teach according to their own educational philosophies. These teachers rated this opportunity lower than did other teacher graduates who had obtained teaching positions. As with the concern regarding adequacy of resources, the principals reported that the PDS teacher-graduates were afforded the opportunity to teach according to their educational philosophies.

Conclusion

The findings from research about this first PDS provide documentation of the value of the PDS experience for university interns, classroom teachers, and students. However, creating this first partnership presented numerous challenges for the university faculty with respect to time commitment and role changes. Overcoming these challenges led to the necessity to experiment with new models and visions of the PDS partnership. Nevertheless, the results of this effort led to funding and support for expansion of PDS partnerships in Maryland. Subsequently, the university was recognized by the Association for Teacher Educators for its innovative programs in teacher education. Reflecting on this early PDS endeavor, it is heartening to note that the school reported on in this chapter remains an active partner with the university in the professional development school network.

CHAPTER THREE

Waverly Elementary School– Towson University Special Education Professional Development School

Debi Gartland & Joyce E. Agness

A Professional Development School has been described as a collaboratively planned and implemented partnership for the academic and clinical preparation of teacher candidates and the continuous professional development of school system and higher education faculty. PDS partnerships are places in which a high-quality education is promoted for all students, including those with disabilities, as well as for teacher candidates, higher education faculty, and school faculty and staff (Abdal-Haqq, 1998; Chance, 2000; Clark, 1999). There is an extensive literature with information on the preparation of general education teacher candidates through the PDS model (Teitel & Abdal-Haqq, 2000), yet, there are few citations on the preparation of special education teacher candidates through the PDS model (Gartland, 2002).

Waverly Elementary School (Howard County Public School System) and Towson University personnel have successfully collaborated to design, implement, and evaluate Maryland's first PDS for Special Education in a neighborhood school. The partnership is exemplary in that it promotes the achievement of rigorous standards by all students, including those with disabilities, supports high-quality academic and clinical preparation for teacher candidates, and provides a mechanism for the simultaneous renewal and continuing professional development of faculty and staff of the school and the university.

The first three years of the Special Education Professional Development School (SPED PDS) partnership are described in this chapter. Specifically, the chapter is about teacher candidate preparation, the on-going professional development of school and university faculty and staff, as well as the challenges unique to a SPED PDS, including lessons learned, modifications made to the SPED PDS based on the lessons learned, and the further evolution of the PDS.

The County Public School System

The Maryland Higher Education Commission (MHEC) and the Maryland State Department of Education (MSDE) have mandated the PDS as the method to be used for the preparation of pre-service teachers and the delivery of professional development to school faculties, administrators, and staff. The Howard County Public School System is working with Towson in implementing that requirement.

The PDS strongly supports at least two goals articulated in the school system's strategic plan. In the Year 2000—Ensuring Excellence in Teaching and Learning, Goal 1 is to ensure that each student meets or exceeds rigorous performance and achievement standards. Goal 2 is to ensure the highest level of performance by all staff. The county believes benefits of a PDS include:

- well-prepared and more confident teachers
- individualized attention and enhanced instruction for children
- enhanced professional development opportunities for faculty and staff
- a pool of well-prepared teacher candidates
- university support for school improvement efforts.

In 1994, the county began its PDS efforts. The then superintendent of schools set a goal for the county to prepare pre-service teachers only through PDS programs. Presently, there are 14 partnerships involving 32 schools ranging from early beginnings programs through high school.

The mission is to employ the collaborative resources of P–12 and higher education to:

- promote the achievement of rigorous standards by all students
- support high-quality academic and clinical training for teacher candidates by providing intensive internship opportunities
- provide a powerful mechanism for the simultaneous renewal and professional development of P–12 and higher education faculties
- serve as centers for the identification and documentation of best practices in teaching and learning through inquiry, research, and reflection
- support efforts to achieve the strategic goals of Beyond the Year 2000.

The HCPSS budget supports a coordinator, two full-time and two part-time staff PDS facilitators as well as school-based site liaisons. The county special education office dedicated a part-time position to the development of SPED PDSs. Within two years of working with the first special education partnership, another partnership was developed and another special education office part time position was added. With the amount of staff devoted to PDS, highly effective communication became especially crucial as special education was an unknown endeavor for most involved. The special education team became a part of the PDS office team.

To better meet the needs of all involved in these PDS partnerships, the county facilitated monthly coordinating council meetings to bring together representatives from all the partnerships. Discussions among college and county representatives precipitated the development of a PDS handbook and a training guide for mentors. With the addition of the special education partnership, discussions broadened to include specification of the needs of general education and special education interns in working with students with disabilities. Additions were made to the training guide to include co-teaching as well as the needs of students with disabilities. All training sessions and discussions have included special education.

The University Special Education Program

Towson University, which graduates the largest number of teacher candidates in the state of Maryland, has been the leader in PDS development in the state. In 1998, Towson began a Bachelor of Science program in Special Education. The satisfactory completion of the major leads to Maryland certification in Generic Special Education at the Infant/Primary level, allowing graduates to teach students with disabilities from birth through grade three. Given the increased emphasis via the Individuals with Disabilities Education Act of 1997 on access to and achievement in the general curriculum for students with disabilities, students with a variety of types and degrees of disabilities are increasingly being educated in more inclusive classes and schools. In order to prepare high-quality personnel who are competent, confident, and ready to face this kind of challenge, the new major was designed to include an intensive, extensive PDS internship.

In November 1998, the possibility of designing the SPED PDS was discussed. The authors of this chapter and other district personnel wrote a grant to develop the SPED PDS. In a subsequent survey, emails were sent to

75 special education faculty members at colleges and universities across the country to locate a PDS model for preparing special education teacher candidates. No such model was found. [Note: In fact, most respondents requested information about progress made with this PDS.] A grant was awarded by MSDE under the Schools for Success/Goals 2000 Program.

Waverly Elementary School

Waverly Elementary School was chosen as the site for the SPED PDS because of its richness of opportunities. At the school, a range of special education programs are well matched to the Towson Infant/Primary major. This is a regular neighborhood school of about 550 students, 75 of whom are part of a Regional Early Childhood Center (RECC). Also, students with mental retardation, autism, and other developmental disabilities from all over the school system are provided an education. Although services and settings are based on individuals' needs, most students are educated in the regular class for the majority of their day with specialists bringing services into regular classrooms.

The grades 1–5 staffing includes three special education teachers, three instructional assistants, a speech and language pathologist, a school psychologist, a part-time occupational therapist, and a part-time physical therapist to serve students with disabilities. A full continuum of special education services is provided, including educating students with disabilities within their own home school population and three regional programs. These programs include:

- a RECC program serving children with disabilities from birth to five years old
- two classes for the deaf and hard-of-hearing students; also, a pilot program for students with cochlear implants
- two classes for students with significant disabilities (including students with severe cognitive impairments and behavioral issues) who are included in the general education classrooms for only part of their day.

This array of programs could provide interns the opportunity to work with students across all disability categories, ranging from mild to severe needs. The school was also chosen because of the strength of the faculty and staff. The special educators are experienced, certified, master teachers who have worked collaboratively with their general education colleagues. In addition, the principal had experience with PDS and was supportive of the partnership.

Presentations about the PDS partnership were made to the special education faculty first and, then, to the entire school faculty and staff, to the PTA, and to the County Board of Education. All groups supported the partnership.

University and County Commitments

The university, the district, and the school each agreed to contribute resources to the development and implementation of the partnership. The university agreed to provide faculty to participate in teaching interns and serving as a resource to the school, as well as support for professional development activities for school faculty and staff, collaboration so school faculty could participate in providing instruction to interns, and on-site graduate courses at greatly reduced tuition and fees. The district agreed to provide continuity in administrative leadership at the school site, a half-time school system position, funding, support for a system-wide governance structure, and preference in interviewing and the hiring of PDS interns. The school agreed to provide commitments to the PDS by the principal, collaboration with the School Improvement Team and faculty, the identification of human resources, including mentors, experiences in the use of technology, sensitivity toward diversity issues and special learning needs, and collegial decision-making. In addition, all three partners committed to the establishment of shared governance and decision-making, the space on site to teach classes to interns, a PDS office with a phone line, and at least a three-year commitment to the PDS.

The Partnership

The partnership between the school and the university is the first known PDS in special education. The experience is a full-year program for interns who have numerous experiences with students of a variety of ages and disabilities along a continuum of service delivery models. The intensive experience immerses the interns into all aspects of the school, resulting in the integration of theory, practice, and evaluation of the experience. Maryland's Essential Dimensions of Teaching as well as INTASC standards are used as the organizing framework for the program. Since the collaboration is focused on special education, the primary performance-based assessments and standards are those of the Council for Exceptional Children, the standards evident in required intern portfolios. At the heart of the PDS is the goal to improve the achievement of students with disabilities. On a continuing basis, data are collected and analyzed in order to implement changes and enhance teacher effectiveness. Ultimately, the focus of the SPED PDS partnership is on improved student performance through research-based teaching and learning.

Benefits

One of the first questions asked by school and district staff when they were approached with this new initiative was "What is in this for students and teachers?" Benefits included those for students, school and district personnel, and university students and faculty. The benefits include:

Students

- Improved student-teacher ratio with the presence of the interns, allowing teachers to work with individual students and providing increased opportunities for students to respond
- Instruction including new best practices
- Higher levels of achievement based upon quarterly assessments.

School Faculty and Staff

- Interns in the classroom, thus providing assistance to teachers and assistants and other staff
- Interns better prepared to teach in classrooms
- Opportunities for on-site graduate and comprehensive professional development (CPD) coursework for free or at reduced tuition and fees.
- Additional CPD credits available for mentoring
- Training and support for mentoring
- Compensation for after-school and Summer PDS planning and workshops
- Opportunities to provide leadership to the PDS
- Opportunities for teaching courses for the university as an adjunct faculty member
- Within school and cross-site collegiality with other PDS partners

- Opportunities to work with higher education faculty and make a contribution to enhancing the teacher education program
- Additional ways to satisfy individual professional development plans
- Opportunities to teach interns and participate in their professional preparation at the PDS site
- Opportunities to attend on-site special education research presentations and receive updates on national legislation and advocacy efforts
- Attend or present at local, regional, and national workshops and conferences
- Availability to utilize the resources of an on-site professional library
- Materials provided to support an on-site professional book club
- Materials provided to support a beginning reading research project
- Professional development on ADHD issues from a national consultant.

University Faculty

- Participation in more authentic training of interns
- Additional time spent in the field versus in university classrooms, thus affording opportunities to remain current with school and district practices
- Enhancing insight into the school system's curricula
- Opportunities to learn and collaborate with school faculty and staff.

The District

- Better-prepared new teachers to hire with a greater opportunity for retaining them
- Knowledge of the interns prior to hiring
- New teachers prepared in their professional education program about district philosophies and practices.

Governance

Joint and shared governance is at the heart of PDS success. Time is required to be able to collaborate in effective ways. In Year 1, the emphasis was on transforming the SPED PDS into a creative and efficient partnership in the absence of a special education PDS model. All of the partners to the PDS were invested in the achievements of the school's students with disabilities as well as the successful preparation of Towson's teacher candidates. In Year 2, mentor needs and schoolwide professional development were the focus of partner's efforts. In Year 3, more activities were added with opportunities to align with the newly developed state PDS standards.

To assure success, collaborative decision-making and effective communication were guideposts. Several groups were formed and activities implemented. These included:

- A Management Committee that consisted of the principal, the district PDS director, and the PDS partnership coordinator for special education, the school site liaison, and the university's SPED PDS coordinator. The members of the committee met monthly and were primarily responsible for overseeing the grant, addressing issues too sensitive to come before the Steering Committee (e.g., employee matters), and planning mentor training.
- A Steering Committee consisting of all the members of the Management Committee as well as other representatives from the school's special education faculty, general education faculty, mentors, parents, and university instructors and interns. The Steering Committee met monthly and decisions were made about mentor selections, intern placements, rotation dates, Fall and Spring Semester experiences, and the site liaison report on monthly mentor meetings.
- Each year a Summer Strategic Planning Institute including Steering Committee representatives and others was held to review the previous year's activities and to plan for the upcoming year. In Year 1, the Institute was held over five days. Major activities included developing syllabi and deciding on content, expectations, experiences, and responsibilities for all partners. For example, a checklist of required experiences, observations, and interview protocol was developed for the Fall Internship. This included interviewing a special education instructional assistant, making a home visit with a RECC teacher, and observing a social group conducted by a school psychologist, guidance counselor, or speech therapist. In subsequent Summer Institutes, fewer days were needed. Time was spent on evaluating what worked well, improving areas in need of change, and planning for increased student achievement.

Mentors, Interns, and the PDS Year

Mentors were selected based on perceived effectiveness, years of experience, tenure, certification, and subjects and populations taught. They were self-nominated or recommended by colleagues, approached only after approval by the principal. The mentors provided orientation for their intern at a welcoming "Tea." During the week prior to students beginning school, mentors shared information on the development of schedules, IEPs and student placement decisions, and how they modeled collaborative planning with general education colleagues. During the Fall semester, they assisted interns in completing the checklist by facilitating observations and conducting interviews as well as supporting the development of lesson plans and initial lesson delivery. During Spring semester, mentors modeled positive teaching practices and supported interns in their increasing responsibilities as well as provided formative and summative feedback in collaboration with the Towson supervisor. The Steering Committee developed a week-by-week enumeration of mentor responsibilities that was attached to the syllabi along with intern responsibilities, thus providing a framework for mutual accountability between mentors and interns.

During Year 1, there were five interns, two of whom were Towson's first two Infant/Primary majors. The other three interns were certification-only students opting to complete the full-year SPED PDS experience instead of the minimal required six weeks of field experiences. During Years 2 and 3, four Infant/Primary majors participated in the program.

The SPED PDS year began in August with interns invited, though not required, to participate in the district's new teacher orientation week activities. Each year, interns took advantage of this opportunity. Also, the interns were required to participate in an on-site Welcoming Tea the day before teachers were required to report back to school. At the Tea, the SPED PDS was described, the upcoming year previewed, and time was given for developing rapport between mentors and interns. The following day, each intern was required to shadow his or her mentor. When the school year began, interns were required to keep mentors' hours at the school with the exception of when they returned to campus for classes. Each year the evaluation data confirm that although interns were initially reluctant to give up part of their summer, they looked back and described these two weeks as being invaluable.

During the Fall semester, the interns were exposed to a variety of students of different ages and disabilities as well as service delivery models. They learned about observations-reflections-guided practice, lesson development and implementation, and data collection and assessment. They took an on-site, three-credit, special education curriculum and methods of classroom management course during the school day taught by a university faculty member. Since the course was on site, interns were afforded the opportunity to bridge theory and practice by taking frequent "field trips" to school classrooms. Several school faculty and district personnel came to these classes as guests to speak on important topics. The interns also took a three-hour internship class on site with an additional three hours of observation and participation at the school each week. The interns were assigned to different mentors for each of their two Fall rotations. After Year 1, it was decided to shift from a 6 week–10 week experience to two 8-week experiences, allowing equal time in a pre-primary (birth–kindergarten) experience and a primary or early elementary (grades 1–3) experience. A university faculty member supervised the Fall Internship.

During the Spring semester, the interns were on site full-time, completing two placements. After Year 1, it was decided to follow an A-B-B-A pattern during the two semesters. The interns spent the first half of the Fall semester with one mentor (A), the second half with their next mentor (B), the first half of Spring semester with their B mentor, and the last half of Spring with their A mentor. This A-B-B-A pattern was developed to ensure a more successful beginning of Spring experience for interns because they were more recently with their B rotation students and knew those students' needs. During mid-March upon returning to the A rotation, the interns were able to see the progress made by students with whom they worked at the beginning of the school year. A university faculty member supervised the Spring internship. Additionally, interns took a three-credit seminar held on-site that assisted in guiding portfolio development, conducting action research, and discussing issues of professional ethics and behavior. School and district personnel visited the seminar and discussed issues of importance related to these topics. For Year 1, the seminar was team-taught by two district special educators. In Year 2, the seminar was team-taught by the university supervisor and the Howard County SPED PDS Coordinator. The Towson supervisor taught the Year 3 seminar. In mid-May, an end-of-year celebration was held with interns showcasing their portfolios and presenting their research projects in roundtable discussion groups.

Existing Challenges

For the mentors, in addition to the challenges any PDS partnership faces, challenges unique to a SPED PDS emerged. In any school, there are a limited number of special educators available to mentor interns; thus, fewer interns can be placed in one school. With the shortage of special educators in Maryland, there are fewer qualified, tenured, certified teachers in schools. Also, master special educators are often afforded leadership positions that limit their direct service with students with disabilities. For example, during the Summer planning week prior to Year 1, two potential mentors were "lost" to promotions with their being re-assigned to other schools. Between Years 1 and 2, another two mentors were lost for similar reasons. Additionally, interns in the birth-kindergarten experience face the challenge of the need for more time in the classroom because the children in those classes come to school for a limited period during the day and for fewer days during the week. Thus, the interns need two mentors during this rotation to make a full-time schedule. Therefore, there is the challenge of having fewer mentors available who may be used repeatedly, in turn, risking "mentor burnout" at a faster rate than mentors in non-SPED PDSs.

For interns, the challenge is in providing as varied an experience as possible. This has meant that when selecting potential schools and mentors, more PDS partnerships will be needed for a sufficient experience. Also, there is a need to find placements in which interns are provided exposure to a range of types of disabilities, levels of severity of disabilities, and ages of students with disabilities. Interns must be placed with mentors who teach a range of content areas and in settings across the continuum. With interns being certified in birth–grade 3, they need to be placed with mentors who serve students in P–3 only.

In terms of resources, although the SPED PDS was pioneering, it was not cost effective. There is a conflict between striving to meet Maryland requirements of having interns in a PDS for 100 days over two consecutive semesters and the pressure from the university to bring courses back on campus if there is not sufficient enrollment in an off-campus site. Whereas the university's other PDS partnerships can have sufficient numbers of interns using two schools for a PDS, in special education, in excess of a dozen schools are needed for the same number of placements. Additionally, there are not enough university special education faculty members to engage in PDS development and implementation. With the increasing numbers of special education majors, there may not be enough PDS sites.

Because our SPED PDS was grant funded, the goal was to demonstrate the increased achievement of students with disabilities on state assessment measures. Data collection was difficult to design. The first priority was to use data from the state assessments. The problem was that the number of students with disabilities taking the tests who had worked with interns would constitute a sample group so small there would not be an impact on scores. Also, the state assessments only provide school scores, not individual scores. It was suggested that growth in terms of the Individualized Education Program (IEP) for each student with disabilities should be used. However, there were too many variables on the IEP for each student and their implementation too varied to use these data to measure increases in achievement. Another issue was on how to measure the effectiveness of early childhood education programming. State tests begin in second grade and county assessments begin in kindergarten. What about the impact on children in pre-kindergarten with whom the interns were working?

The members of the Steering Committee decided to use the state testing data in addition to the quarterly data collected by the school for each student. Then, the progress of students could be examined in relationship to the curriculum and to those students assigned interns. When looking at achievement in the early childhood setting, it was decided to use the early childhood checklist of skills. After Year 2, only these data seemed to be a reliable measure. An overall upward trend was shown for the year. However, the overall results on state assessments remained relatively flat rather than closing the gap or increasing it, as had been hoped. Many factors may have contributed to this. First, several students whose scores contributed to these results were new to the school. Therefore, there may not have been any cumulative benefits for those students. Second, there was a great deal of turnover in the school's special education department; thus, professional development gains within the individual special education faculty were lost. Third, the interns were new each year. Thus, it may be difficult to predict any cumulative benefit to student achievement that could be attributed to the program. On the positive side, there are many more staff benefiting professionally from PDS professional development activities, and the higher expectations held for staff may have contributed toward maintaining student gains even with the high turnover of staff.

Lessons Learned

A SPED PDS is an avenue to bright futures for all participants. Students with disabilities are supported more in inclusive settings and are achieving at higher rates on quarterly assessments than pre-PDS. The SPED PDS interns who graduate from the program have been highly sought after as new teachers, and principals report that as first-year teachers these graduates seem more like second-year teachers because of the intensive, extensive PDS internship. Additionally, the SPED PDS has supported and helped to retain the school's faculty and staff, providing a variety of rewards for all involved. With no SPED PDS models existing, rules were developed as time passed, reinforcing that flexibility is key in special education. A number of other lessons were learned.

- Collaborative decision-making and effective communication is essential to the success of a PDS.
- Monthly meetings of Management and Steering Committees are critical for effective communication and a smoothly running partnership.
- Mentor training needs to be scheduled at a convenient day, time, and place for optimal participation.
- Training must be based on an assessment of needs and open to all current and prospective mentors.
- Effective use of substitute teachers allowed mentors to be freed up for planning and to attend and present at professional conferences.
- University and district staff can influence each other's programs in positive ways.
- A PDS has to involve professional development for all in a school and all partners.
- While this school was an optimal place to prepare SPED PDS interns, it cannot initially reap benefits unless the principal hires special educators who can mentor newly minted graduates of the SPED PDS or the PDS will not be ready for three years or so.
- Providing identification to the PDS, [for example, SPED PDS polo shirts with a collaboratively created design and motto ("A Special PDS")] is one way to build a community of learners among the PDS partners.

Local, State, and National Recognition

As the first SPED PDS at a regular, neighborhood school in Maryland and possibly the nation, the partnership has received local, regional, and national recognition. In April 2001, the Maryland Association of Teacher Educators' 2001 Honoree Award for Distinguished Partnerships in Teacher Education was presented to the PDS partners.

With the award came invitations to speak at three conferences. Also, there were requests to provide testimony to an MSDE Teacher Preparation Subcommittee and to present to other state groups. SPED PDS interns, general educators, and parents have presented with university and school administrators and special educators and district PDS staff. Additionally, various aspects of the SPED PDS have been presented at nine national conferences, including those of the American Educational Research Association, the Council for Exceptional Children (CEC), CEC's Teacher Education Division, CEC's Division on Mental Retardation/Developmental Disabilities, and the National PDS Conference sponsored by MSDE in 2003.

Evolution

After three successful years as a SPED PDS, the Management and Steering Committees decided to "vacation" the special education mentors. The SPED PDS merged with a two-year-old university elementary education PDS comprised of two elementary schools within five miles of the school. This PDS was seeking opportunities for additional general education mentors along with additional special education mentors to avoid burnout. With the approval of the university's Special Education Major at the elementary level, it was decided to expand to include special education teacher candidates seeking certification in grades 1–8. Currently, this effort is in the second year at a three-school partnership with special education and elementary education PDS interns at all three schools.

References

Abdal-Haqq, I. (1998). *Professional development schools: Weighing the evidence*. Thousand Oaks, CA: Corwin Press.

Chance, L. (Ed.) (2000). *Professional development schools: Combining school improvement and teacher preparation*. Washington, DC: National Education Association.

Clark, R.W. (Ed.) (1999).*Effective professional development schools: Weighing the evidence*. San Francisco: Jossey-Bass.

Gartland, D. (2002). Assuring better outcomes for students through special education professional development school. Presentation at the 24th Annual International Conference of the Teacher Education Division of the Council for Exceptional Children, Savannah, GA.

Teitel, L., & Abdal-Haqq, I. (2000). *Assessment: Assessing the impacts of professional development schools.* Washington, DC: American Association of Colleges for Teacher Education.

CHAPTER FOUR

Defining Our Own Roles: Professional Renewal for Teachers and University Faculty

Cynthia Hartzler-Miller & Terri Wainwright

Introduction

Throughout the PDS literature, educators use the phrase "simultaneous reform" or "simultaneous renewal" to highlight the call for systemic changes in
schools and universities. Darling-Hammond, Bullmaster & Cobb (1995), for
instance, define professional development schools as "collaborations between schools and universities that have been created to support the learning
of prospective and experienced teachers while *simultaneously restructuring*
schools and schools of education" (p. 88, emphasis added). In the Maryland
State Department of Education (2001) manual for statewide PDS implementation, the following is proclaimed, "PDSs provide the foundation for the *simultaneous renewal* of teacher education and schools" (p. i, emphasis
added). This vision for simultaneous reform is broad, multi-layered, and
radical in the sense that it challenges traditional roles and norms. PDSs are
intended to change the way schools and universities prepare new teachers
and to transform the nature and organization of teachers' and teacher-
educators' work (Abdal-Haqq, 1998; Carnegie Forum, 1996; Goodlad, 1990;
Holmes Group, 1986, 1990, 1995).

One component of simultaneous reform redefines the roles of univer-
sity- and school-based faculty. Unlike traditional professors of education
who visit schools only to observe student teachers, university-based PDS
faculty divide their time equally between sites:

> Sometimes they teach classes on campus, as professors have always done, and
> other times they provide professional development for practicing educators at the
> PDS itself through study groups and other means. Sometimes they co-teach chil-
> dren in the public school; other times they confer with school teams as part of

their shared responsibility for interns. They spend some of their time at the PDS testing hypotheses through action- and intervention-oriented research projects, carrying out this work alone at times and sometimes collaborating with school faculty members. (Holmes Group, 1995, p. 60)

And in contrast to the static teaching assignments and limited professional growth opportunities in a typical school, field-based PDS teachers "are full colleagues of the university-based faculty, partners in a renewal of professional education based on integrating practice with theory" (The Holmes Group, 1995, p. 63). PDS teachers are regarded as leaders in their field, serious professionals whose expertise gives them access to a wide variety of roles: classroom and university instructor, new teacher mentor, developer of curriculum, researcher, assessment specialist, and school-community liaison.

To anyone familiar with the status quo in schools and universities, simultaneous reform is about radical change. Yet as Teitel (1997) has observed, neither schools nor universities are typically receptive to "high stakes/high impact" decisions. It is more likely, especially in a new PDS, partners will gravitate toward "low stakes/low impact changes," leaving existing roles and relationships intact. For example, PDSs are sometimes criticized by reformers for accomplishing little more than increasing the number of student teachers at a single school when university-based faculty members work with school-based coordinators to arrange field placements with no fundamental changes in the nature of their roles or responsibilities (Clark, 1999; Goodlad, 1995).

School and university faculty may be at a stage in their careers when they are searching for the kinds of opportunities promised by simultaneous reform. Researchers in teacher career development and professional life cycles call attention to the gap between experienced teachers' desires for professional renewal and the limited opportunities typically available to them (Fessler & Christensen, 1992; Huberman, 1989). They note, "what is critical for teachers during this period of their lives and careers is the opportunity for renewal to occur that is experimental and novel in nature and under their own control. This sort of development implies that teachers will find themselves in a flexible environment with sufficient resources to experiment and to succeed as well as fail" (Fessler & Christensen, 1992, p.172). Although far less research exists on the career development of university faculty, several autobiographical case studies document the need for professional renewal in teacher-educators' professional lives (Bullough, 1997; Chin, 1997; Chin &

Russell, 1996; Elijah, 1996; Finley, 1996; Russell, 1997). Elijah (1996), for example, uses bell hooks's (1994) phrase "engaged pedagogy" to refer to teacher-educators' need to interact meaningfully with classroom teachers and their students as part of a "process of self-actualization that promotes their own well-being" (cited in Elijah, 1996, p. 86).

There may be a fit, theoretically, between the structural and organizational changes proposed by simultaneous reform and the professional renewal needs of university and school faculty. In practice, the question of "fit" is context dependent. Every professional development school contains pre-existing structures (defined roles, hierarchies of authority, communication patterns) and unique individuals' histories, values and aspirations— whether, how and what kind of change happens hinges on those particular stakeholders' interpretations of events and the meanings they co-construct (Fullan, 2001).

Since simultaneous reform results in a transformation of professional educators' roles and relationships, it is necessary to take into account how teachers view their work, define their professional goals and needs, and interpret change. This chapter is an examination of the perspectives of university- and school-based faculty members in the first year of a professional development school partnership involving a university, a middle school, and a high school. There are two key informants. One, Terri, is a 20-year veteran high school English teacher who serves as one of the school-based PDS site coordinators. The other, Cynthia, is a university professor with six years of experience as a high school social studies teacher and seven years as a teacher-educator who is the university-based site facilitator. The two informants consider the ways in which their own and their colleagues' motivations, values, and expectations interact with existing and new structures within their personal PDS context.

Data and Methods

The study was designed to explore the multiple perspectives of various stakeholders as the design and implementation of the PDS unfolded. The methodological orientation is phenomenological. In other words, it is assumed that reality is socially constructed as each of us creates meaning from ordinary, daily experiences and, through careful listening, discerns multiple ways of interpreting events. Beginning with the initial meetings between university and school personnel, the formation of a cross-institutional PDS

Steering Committee and the arrival of the first cohort of 14 interns, we attempted to document words and actions in minutes, surveys, and interviews. In addition, semi-structured interviews were conducted with eight teachers, one parent, two principals, and three university professors.

Rather than approach the data with preconceived categories, inductive, comparative analysis was used to identify themes and patterns as well as divergent or unique perspectives (Bogdan & Biklen, 1998; Glaser & Strauss (1967). Although the work in this chapter is based solely upon data collected during the first year of the PDS, in subsequent years we will return to the same study participants to document changes in perceptions over time. Preservice teachers and middle/high school students also will be included in the next round of data collection.

Professional Renewal

During the first five months of the partnership, minutes from PDS Steering Committee meetings and faculty presentations revealed that explicit attention was given to the planning of the internship program. We regard this five-month period in Teitel's (1997) terms as "low stakes/low impact" decision-making. We did not explicitly challenge existing roles and relationships. The primary goal was to plan and implement the interns' schedule of seminars, observations, and teaching.

When reviewing interview transcripts we noticed the potential for more radical change. Several teachers and university faculty perceived the partnership as something more than an extended internship for novices. It seemed that a driving force generating interest and commitment to the PDS was teachers' felt need to grow and change in their profession in a direction that seemed different from traditional, administrative roles. Some veteran teachers viewed traditional opportunities for professional renewal as undesirable. The role of school administrator, department chair, or county curriculum supervisor removed them from the work they cared for the most: experiencing the classroom, interacting with students, and perfecting the art of facilitating learning. They expressed feelings of being "stifled" and "disconnected" from fellow teachers when within the professional confines dictated by central office agendas. While some teachers had moved into university or community college teaching positions, this option was unappealing to others who were committed to the secondary school environment.

These master teachers who are knowledgeable and experienced in classroom management, questioning, assessment, and communicating with students represent a vast resource of expertise. Some veteran teachers feel the need for professional renewal, but the available options separate them from work environments in which their expertise is best utilized and energizes their practice. They see the PDS as a venture into new professional territory, an opportunity to create new roles for themselves as mentors of new teachers.

Three components of this new role were identified which emerged from the surveys and interviews. The first component, "teaching novices," is a focus on the mentors' pedagogical decisions in relation to the perceived needs of new teachers. The second component is "collaborating with teachers," involving opportunities to work directly with colleagues. The third component is "influencing teacher education," relating to the broader issue of attracting and supporting high-quality teacher candidates.

This new professionally renewing role for teachers is interesting in that there is a sharing with the university facilitator role. For example, simultaneously, Cynthia was trying to create a similar role for herself. Although she has a doctorate in teacher education, curriculum, and educational policy, she has never stopped thinking like a high school social studies teacher. She is passionate about subject content as well as the development of young adolescents. A school building is familiar, comfortable territory. At the same time, she thrives in a university setting where the access to books and intellectual discourse is invigorating. She finds, personally and professionally, she needs to maintain an inner dialogue between scholarship and practice. The PDS model creates opportunities for Cynthia to fashion an alternative role that is professionally renewing because it brings together her various interests and values.

Teaching Novices

Throughout the year, we tried to assess the willingness of school faculty to work with the interns, first through a survey (Fall 2001) and, then, through individual requests for support of interns as needed. On the initial survey, participants were asked to what degree a faculty member wished to be involved. Almost all of the surveys returned indicated some interest and desire to be involved in the PDS. The degree of participation ranged from a minimal willingness to be observed to an eager desire to participate in all aspects of the internship.

Site coordinators at both schools involved a great number of faculty colleagues in a variety of tasks and activities. These include:

- being observation models for interns
- supervising and mentoring classroom and laboratory experiences as interns engage in "bit teaching" and student teaching
- demonstrating technology integration in instruction and other aspects of schooling
- participating with students in service projects
- serving as action research advisors
- providing expertise on special programs (special education, guidance, assessment, reading, administration, interviewing, portfolio preparation)
- participating on new and experienced teacher panels
- evaluating intern portfolios.

The high school-based teachers were drawn into working directly with interns because of the chance to put their many years of experience to use. In the past, schools had hosted one to three student teachers each year from different teacher training programs and were somewhat randomly placed in classrooms. The low-level change to accommodate 10 to 15 interns seemed to stimulate veteran teachers to think more about how they could best instruct, support, and encourage interns and facilitate their learning experience. Each time Terri talked with the faculty as a group or individually, she noticed the energy and enthusiasm with which her colleagues responded. Many made practical suggestions, gave offers of help, suggested speakers, and provided general encouragement. Others sent copies of pertinent articles they thought we could use.

Some teachers in interviews talked about a "rubbing-off" effect, feeling reinvigorated by the interns' enthusiasm:

> The positive for veteran teachers is the excitement that the PDS interns bring, that teaching is new and they're ready to meet new challenges and are very enthusiastic. That has a positive impact on veteran teachers, when you can look back and say, "That's where I used to be." Not that they've lost that, but looking back and thinking, "They're so excited" and some of that excitement is rubbing off. (Teacher Interview, 6/10/02)

Other teachers viewed the experience of mentoring interns as an opportunity to examine their own teaching:

> It creates a situation where our best practices are to be put forward, to be examined and reexamined. Just the presence of [interns] is an opportunity for everybody to grow, because that's what they're trying to do. The goal of the interns is to learn what teaching is about. That makes us examine our practices, to develop ourselves. (Teacher Interview, 6/6/02)

Cynthia's interest in mentoring pre-service teachers was sparked in her fourth year of teaching social studies in high school. During that year, there were four student teachers in the school who had virtually been abandoned by their cooperating teachers. Cynthia and a colleague, remembering their own struggles to "sink or swim," invited the student teachers to join them for informal after-school meetings at a local restaurant. Surprisingly, Cynthia found these interactions to be renewing, allowing her to articulate her own sense of good practice to interns. She began to envision a career in which she would facilitate reflective conversations among new teachers to help them look closely at their own practice, their interactions with students, and their representations of subject matter as part of the process of learning to teach. In contrast to the typical university-based teacher-educator who spends minimal time in schools, Cynthia's PDS role puts her in the classrooms where interns are learning to teach so she can make direct observations and hold individual and group sessions on topics such as differentiating instruction, multiculturalism, and classroom management.

Collaborating with Teachers and University Faculty

We were surprised at the extent the high school teachers experienced renewal through their collaboration in the PDS. As one teacher put it:

> There are different types of schools. I've been reading lately about the legacy of the one-room school; in [some schools] teachers are still very, very isolated.... We are moving from being a conventional school to being a very collegial school. We're encouraging professional dialogue, sharing information, opening your classroom door, letting more people come in and see what you're doing, involving teachers in inquiry groups, asking good questions, examining data. It's a very reflective place to be. And having interns in the school generates that. (Teacher Interview, 6/10/02)

While Cynthia had taught high school in the isolated environment of the "conventional" school model, she had been frustrated by attempts to initiate professional discussions with her colleagues about theories and principles of teaching and learning. In graduate school, she learned about the PDS model and felt drawn to the growing emphasis on collaborative study groups.

The desire for collaboration and professional dialogue was a source of creativity and innovation. Whether meetings were informal, spontaneous gatherings in the faculty lounge or formal sessions of the PDS Steering Committee, new ideas were generated. Together, we identified, discussed, and worked on issues such as "How can we get our interns to lead more meaningful classroom discussions?" "What kind of data would show us what 7th graders are actually learning from their Skills for Success class?" Then, we implemented new ideas: videotaping discussions led by master teachers, conducting action research projects, sharing responsibility for observing interns' teaching, engaging in after-school chat sessions with new teachers, and sponsoring mentoring workshops. Together, we collaborated on presentations about our work at a national conference and in a university graduate course.

Terri's relationships with colleagues were enhanced by the PDS. The formal requirements of the site coordinator position involved keeping all parties informed, contacting teachers, arranging observations, creating schedules for bit teaching, and following up with teachers and interns. In short, she was the liaison for interns, university faculty, administrative personnel, and classroom teachers. Unintentionally, she became a "mentor" to her peers. They asked her for advice about how to integrate interns into the classroom, how to deal with struggling interns, and how to write the final intern evaluations. Her colleagues invited her to come into their classrooms, observe interns, evaluate their performance, and talk about best practices. This was professionally renewing for her, in the sense that her professional experience was being acknowledged and used in a way it had never been before.

Terri noted a marked improvement in morale among the teachers in her school since the PDS began. Informally, teachers shared their feeling of being valued for their professional contribution, of having their expertise appreciated and acknowledged by interns, peers, administrators, and university personnel. Some of them suggested that for the first time they felt like "true professionals," who are trusted to know their craft, are consulted about their techniques, and acknowledged for their mastery, originality, and experience. One of the administrators underscored this point in her interview:

> I loved the meeting where [site coordinators, mentor teachers, and university faculty] came together. I guess this is going to sound weird, but school-based staff are not treated as professionals. Unless you go out and seek that, you'll never have it. But [at that meeting] the teachers were validated professionally, we were all educators with experience...looking at what we can do to support learning for kids (Administrator Interview, 6/6/02)

Reforming Teacher Education

It appears to many of the high school teachers that fewer and fewer individuals are entering the teaching profession. Of those who do, fewer are among the intellectually gifted, and fewer will make it through the first five years of teaching. Other less demanding professions and jobs offer more money, better benefits, and better hours. Yet, the problem of new teacher retention is made more complicated by falling on the university and the individual school system levels to provide realistic preparation, support, continuing instruction, and mentoring opportunities that are present in most other professions. Often novice teachers are left on their own to sink or swim.

In Terri's conversations with colleagues when attempting to recruit them as mentor teachers, the interaction often included topics such as what veteran teachers owe the profession and how they could positively influence the interns and the university teacher training program. They expressed concerns about the teacher shortage and what it means to the future of their own school's teaching staff. At the high school about one-third of the faculty is near retirement age. They worry about the quality of new teachers who will replace them. Because of this immediate and ongoing concern, teachers and administrators are particularly attuned to the national crisis in locating and keeping teaching candidates. One of the principals lamented the lack of quality teacher candidates:

> The most challenging part of my job is keeping good teachers in the classrooms. That's what it's all about. I could be the greatest principal in the world and if we don't have good teachers, this is not going to be a successful school. I could be a rotten principal, but with good teachers, the school would be effective....Like

for example, [the district-level math supervisor] was in the other day and she's really concerned. If I had a math vacancy right now, she doesn't have any good candidates....Now we're having mid-year resignations. That is becoming the norm, [whereas] in the past, no one would have done that. (Administrator Interview, 5/16/02)

Teachers and administrators viewed the PDS as an opportunity to influence teacher education to an extent that had previously been unavailable to them. The traditional model of teacher preparation keeps school personnel at arm's length with teacher candidates spending much more time at the university in courses rather than in classrooms. Mentor teachers are not expected to provide direct instruction to novices. In the PDS model interns are brought into the schools for 20 days in the first semester and 80 days in the second semester. School-based PDS faculty are heavily involved in reforming pre-service teacher preparation because they are so involved in it. One theme in the interviews related to teacher education reform was the idea that in a PDS novices develop teaching skills and knowledge sooner because the process is more nurturing than in a traditional program:

The way most teachers here [learned to teach] was [in programs where] they just throw you in. When I was doing my student teaching, my cooperating teacher said "Watch me for a week," then he watched me for a week, and then he said "Give me your lesson plans every Monday for the full teaching load starting the following week."...The PDS is an excellent way of taking those people who would like to be a teacher and gradually bringing them into the culture of the school so they can craft a philosophy and begin to practice it in their student teaching. It's a graduated system of mentoring and nurturing those people who would like to be teachers. (Teacher Interview, 6/10/02)

One of the principals was very specific about the developmental stages of learning to teach:

The most intimidating thing in [learning to teach] is walking in and [confronting] the fact that "I'm not the teacher." At what point do you take on that role that "I am the teacher?" In the PDS, [you get to that point] sooner. You build that relationship with your mentor teacher [in the first semester] so that teacher trusts you and you trust that teacher. I think that when that happens, you go with it. [By the second semester], the teachers and students are familiar faces...so that part is done and you can get a lot more teaching experience. (Administrator Interview, 6/6/02)

A second theme related to teacher education reform involves changing the content of university courses to include language and stories from the daily lives of teachers and students:

> [PDS] gives the university access to the school....It gives [the university faculty member] more access to what's happening today in terms of learning, high school assessments, and school climate. When [the university faculty member] is in the school building, you know what you see when you walk in and you can go back to your students and teach what you see. If [the university faculty member] wasn't here and part of us, [she'd] be teaching all that in isolation of what (the school) is all about. (Administrator Interview, 6/6/02)

It is common for university education programs to be criticized for separating theory from practice. PDSs enable school and university faculty to challenge that false dichotomy where it exists. Spending sustained, meaningful time in schools forces Cynthia to situate her theoretical understandings in practice and enriches her language and images of teaching and learning. She carries this language and these images back to the university where they find their way into discussions with non-PDS colleagues within her department.

For example, the department has relied on bit teaching as a strategy to initiate students into the teaching role. Prospective teachers bit teach several times during their first two semesters in the program. After working with interns and mentor teachers, it has become apparent that bit teaching has limited value. It may be a means to ensure interns have exposure to students, but novices cannot integrate theory and practice (developing meaningful lesson plans, managing classroom time and materials, and responding to the needs of a unique group of learners) unless they work with the same content and students over an extended period of time. At the PDS site, there has been an initiative to make a slight adjustment in the first-semester program by increasing the amount of time spent with a single mentor teacher from two class periods to five each during the days the intern is on-site.

Discussion

The new structures of the PDS partnership—a two-semester internship for a cohort of 10–15 interns with the appointment of a one third-time university liaison and site coordinators, the creation of a cross-institutional Steering Committee—were designed to facilitate low stakes/low impact change. That is, this effort facilitated communication among stakeholders and helped to channel human and material resources where needed. Behind the scenes, teachers and teacher-educators were forming their own interpretations of events, co-constructing new roles that incorporated their own professional interests and dreams, which, in turn, generated new ideas for programmatic change and teacher education reform.

It is hard to say exactly when or how systemic change within the PDS began. Perhaps it was the simple act of calling teachers "mentors" rather than "cooperating teachers" that triggered a new self-consciousness and an interest in redefining professional roles. Certainly, direct contact with interns provided concrete pedagogical issues around which to develop these new roles. In formal and informal conversations with each other, Cynthia, Terri, and veteran teachers deliberated over questions such as: When should the interns start teaching? How much of the lesson should we have them teach? Should we do certain things for interns or expect them to be independent? Should we provide interns with feedback up front or give them more time to practice and make mistakes? What is the best kind of feedback to give interns when they are just starting out, as opposed to later, when they have had more experience in the classroom? Perhaps all of us were invigorated by thinking about these questions because they empowered us to draw upon our pedagogical expertise, our subject matter knowledge, and our commitment to secondary students and the profession.

We also observed that as teachers collectively and individually reflected on their practice, the continual presence of interns in the school strengthened their opinion of themselves as professionals. Although teachers are experts in education, content, and child or adolescent behavior, only their students typically observe them demonstrate that expertise. In addition, the public perception of the teaching profession seems to chip away at teachers' self-esteem. In the PDS, though, teachers are constantly invited to share their expertise with interns and peers, thus providing a more public validation of their professional knowledge and skills.

Whatever the initial cause, we view the desire for professional renewal to be a driving force within the PDS partnership. It is a grassroots phenomenon. Those at the top, educational policymakers and school administrators, are more often oriented toward student achievement rather than teacher development. At the university, the usual expectation is for faculty to teach courses on campus and conduct research. Both stakeholders are conscious of the pressure to sacrifice professional interests, but through the PDS, we have been able to inject our own sincere and needs-based perspectives into the PDS and into the preparation of new teachers. Thus, we have defined our own new roles.

It is precisely because we are defining our professional selves, rather than accepting the definitions imposed by others, that professional renewal does challenge existing power structures. Our experience suggests that when teachers and university faculty define their own roles, creative energy is generated, new ideas are formed, and old ways of doing things are questioned. At her school, Terri assumed some of the principal's authority to assign mentor teachers and work with newly hired teachers. This has enabled her to select mentor teachers for their instructional expertise and draw upon teachers' first-hand knowledge to design an effective new teacher induction program.

This kind of "power shift" is evident when we consider that professional renewal naturally has taken us into the arena of teacher education reform, meaning a sharing with the university of the control of its programs. Two issues, then, have emerged to date: one concerns control over the decision to permit an intern's early release from the program (in instances where an intern has been offered a teaching contract before the internship has been completed), and the other involves the practice of hiring non-PDS university faculty to serve as university supervisors. In regard to the first issue, teachers were able to persuade the university to adopt a more inclusive decision-making process. From now on, the early release of interns will only be granted if school-based PDS faculty members in partnership with the university faculty provide their consent. As for the second issue, the PDS Steering Committee has had to be more subversive. That is, unable to replace traditional university supervisors with more reform-minded professionals, we entreat them to attend mentoring workshops in order to increase their awareness of PDS goals and expectations.

Regardless of the hurdles that must be faced as a result of challenging existing power structures, we believe more radical reform is possible in the PDS partnership. Thus, there is no turning back from the new definitions that have been given to professional roles. The power of our own interpretations and search for meaning cannot be undone. We collect our "data" on a daily basis and make our own judgments about teacher education. We observe the difficult transition interns must make from college student to teacher, and we see how theory and practice come together in a veteran teacher's classroom. Our context-specific and locally responsive PDS experience shines a spotlight on this work, causing us to see ourselves and what we do more clearly. We envision a future PDS characterized by a nurturing professional environment where pre-service and veteran teachers become facilitators of learning while renewing their own professional goals.

References

Abdal-Haqq, I. (1998). *Professional development schools: Weighing the evidence.* Thousand Oaks, CA: Corwin Press.

Bogdan, R.C. & Biklen, S.K. (1998). *Qualitative research for education: An introduction to theory and methods.* Boston: Allyn and Bacon.

Bullough Jr., R.V. (1997). Practicing theory and theorizing practice in teacher education. In J. Loughran & T. Russell (Eds.), *Teaching about teaching: Purpose, passion and pedagogy in teacher education* (pp. 13–31). London: Falmer Press.

Carnegie Forum on Education and the Economy (1996). *A nation prepared: Teachers for the 21st century.* Washington, DC: Author.

Chin, P. (1997). Teaching and learning in teacher education: Who is carrying the ball? In J. Loughran & T. Russell (Eds.), *Teaching about teaching: Purpose, passion and pedagogy in teacher education* (pp. 117–130). London: Falmer Press.

Chin, P. & Russell, T. (1996). Reforming teacher education: Making sense of our past to inform our future. *Teacher Education Quarterly, 23,* 55–68.

Clark, R.W. (1999). *Effective professional development schools.* San Francisco:Jossey-Bass.

Darling-Hammond, L, Bullmaster, M.L. & Cobb, V.L. (1995). Rethinking teacher leadership through professional development schools. *The Elementary School Journal, 96,* 87–106.

Elijah, R. (1996). Professional lives, institutional contexts: Coherence and contradictions. *Teacher Education Quarterly, 23,* 69–90.

Fessler, R. & Christensen, J.D. (1992). *The teacher career cycle: Understanding and guiding the professional development of teachers.* Boston: Allyn and Bacon.

Finley, S. (1996). Professional lives in context: Becoming teacher educators. *Teacher Education Quarterly, 23,* 91–107.

Fullan, M. (2001). *The new meaning of educational change.* New York: Teachers College Press.

Glaser, B.G. & Strauss, A.L. (1967). *The discovery of grounded theory: Strategies for qualitative research.* Chicago: Aldine Publishing.

Goodlad, J. I. (1990). *Teachers for our nation's schools.* San Francisco: Jossey-Bass.

Goodlad, J. I. (1995). School-university partnerships and partner schools. In H.S. Petrie (Ed.), *Professionalization, partnership, and power: Building professional development schools.* Albany: State University of New York Press.

Holmes Group (1986). *Tomorrow's teachers.* East Lansing, MI: Author.

Holmes Group (1990). *Tomorrow's schools: Principles for the design of professional development schools.* East Lansing, MI: Author.

Holmes Group (1995). *Tomorrow's schools of education.* East Lansing, MI: Author.

hooks, b. (1994). *Teaching to transgress: Education as the practice of freedom.* New York: Routledge.

Huberman, M. (1989). The professional life cycle of teachers. *Teachers College Record, 91,* 31–58.

Maryland State Department of Education (2001). *PDS Implementation Manual.* Baltimore, MD: Author.

Russell, T. (1997). Teaching teachers: How I teach IS the message. In J. Loughran & T. Russell (Eds.), *Teaching about teaching:Purpose, passion and pedagogy in teacher education* (pp. 32–47). London: Falmer Press.

Teitel, L. (1997). The organization and governance of professional development schools. In M. Levine & R. Trachtman (Eds.), *Making professional development schools work: Politics, practice and policy* (pp. 115–133). New York: Teachers College Press.

CHAPTER FIVE

"You Want Us to Do What?"
The Story of the Conversion
of a Secondary Education Faculty
to the Professional Development
School Movement[1]

Gloria A. Neubert, James B. Binko, & Sally J. McNelis

In 1995, the Maryland Higher Education Commission mandated that "every teacher candidate...do an extensive internship in a specially designed Professional Development School" (p. 2), and "school-university partnerships must address the initial preparation and continuing education needs of teaching interns, beginning teachers, and experienced educators at various stages of their careers" (p. 11). Specifically, the partnerships are to be reciprocal with university faculty participating in the professional development schools by "teaching on-site courses and seminars for teacher candidates and experienced teachers, involvement in school improvement projects, participation in site-based research projects, and service on mentoring and assessment teams" (p. 20).

1996—The Question

This mandate presented a challenge to Towson University's Department of Secondary Education, whose teacher candidates are liberal arts majors (social studies, English, math, science, foreign language, etc.) and complete teacher certification requirements (32 credits) as a track, not as a major. The members of the faculty have limited control in blocking the time of the candidates. The performance of teacher candidates is quite high as indicated from reports by mentor teachers in the schools and subsequent employers. This raises a question about other research results of the performance of students participating in professional development schools for a majority of their professional preparation.

According to Teitel (1996), there have been few quantitative studies of professional development schools. He also noted there have been several attitudinal studies in which positive results have been demonstrated regarding expectations of the PDS experience or satisfaction with the PDS experience (p. 29), but only Stallings (1991) used multiple quantitative and qualitative measures to determine the positive effectiveness of a PDS model on teacher candidate classroom performance. Given the high regard for graduates of the before implementation of PDS in Secondary Education but the limited data about effectiveness, the Secondary Education faculty at Towson were interested in investigation of the PDS prior to implementation of the state requirement.

The efficacy of the department's approach to PDS as an alternative systemic and simultaneous reform of teacher education was tested. Since early on in the development of the PDS model at Towson, beginning in 1995, reciprocity and exchange with partner school staff have been at the center of the work being done. Therefore, at each PDS site, extensive professional development opportunities have been provided on an on-going basis in return for the opportunity to provide classes and practicum and internship opportunities on school sites. The effectiveness of professional development efforts was determined as well.

In Spring 1996, Secondary Education faculty approached Eastern Technical High School, a comprehensive magnet school in Baltimore County, about becoming a pilot PDS site for English and Social Studies majors. Eastern was chosen because of the history between the Humanities Department Chair and one of the Secondary Education faculty members. For many years, they had taught together in another public school, conducted collaborative research, written and presented at conferences, and worked together regularly as cooperating teacher and university supervisor. Also, this high school teacher was invested in playing a significant role in training the next generation of teachers. Having positive, practicing teaching models is a "must" for successful PDS experiences and effective professional preparation of teacher candidates, and Eastern Technical teachers and staff were excellent models of teaching as well as mirroring the "best" professional practices as career educators. In addition, the principal and assistant principal had a history of being effective educational leaders as well as wanting to have the PDS at their school.

Eastern is a school with students from medium- and low-income families, and many students would be first-generation high school graduates. There is a significant emphasis on inclusionary practices for students with disabilities. Since Towson was investing heavily in new instructional technologies, the school is technologically advanced due to partnerships with local businesses. These factors, then, made Eastern a favorable setting for the university's entry into Secondary Education PDS efforts.

Upon the agreement between Eastern Technical High School and Towson's Department of Secondary Education, a strategic planning committee was established. Membership included the department chair, a secondary education professor who was to serve as the department's PDS coordinator, another secondary education professor who was to focus on the evaluation of the pilot effort, Eastern's humanities chair who would be the on-site PDS coordinator, the associate principal, two social studies teachers, and two English teachers. During an intensive weeklong Summer workshop, the members of the committee, assisted via cameo visits from parents, students, support personnel as well as other Eastern Technical and university faculty members, designed the PDS internship experience and planned professional development activities for members of both faculties.

The PDS pilot project began in September 1996 with 11 English and social studies student interns reporting to Eastern for an elective, 3-credit, differentiated student teaching course that became known as "internship." The course was offered on Tuesday mornings during the semester prior to the student teaching semester. The interns, who were simultaneously enrolled in their discipline-specific methods course (i.e., Teaching English in the Secondary School or Teaching Social Studies in the Secondary School) as well as courses in their subject area major, had volunteered for this elective course.

The internship course was team-taught by the chair of Secondary Education and the humanities chair at the high school. It was conducted in a "teaching hospital" format with each session beginning with an overview of the specific focus for the day, followed by visits to classrooms to observe, assist or teach, followed by a debriefing with the host classroom teachers and other faculty and staff for reflective discussions. The course focus was on performance outcomes associated with 1) classroom management and discipline, 2) applications of technology to teaching, and, 3) reflection on teaching. These topics were chosen because these skills can more readily be learned on site, rather than on the university campus. During the last three weeks of the course, the interns worked with mentor teachers in the classes in which they would be student teaching the following semester. Pre-service peer coaching was also included in the course.

Reciprocity is at the core of Towson's PDS partnerships. Another aspect of the interns' training and a way to assist in enhancing the educational environment and program for Eastern's students was the participation of the interns in service projects at the school. These projects were a way of "giving back" to the school for the mentoring provided to them. The interns selected from a lengthy list of service activities, such as tutoring individual students who have not passed mandatory state tests, accompanying students on field trips to plays and museums, monitoring students during lunch in the cafeteria, attending site-based management meetings, and assisting Eastern faculty with newspaper, yearbook, and drama productions. Each student arranged the time at the school to participate in these activities.

Interestingly, eight Eastern teachers attended the internship course with the interns, thereby extending the reach of the PDS program directly to school faculty. Because Eastern Technical High School is a magnet school for students interested in pursuing technical fields, some faculty with specific technical expertise (e.g., engineers, graphic designers, chemical technicians) are hired directly from the workplace. These faculty members were not schooled in pedagogy and were seeking teacher certification concurrent with their teaching at Eastern. Substitutes were hired each Tuesday so these teachers could attend the course in the morning and, then, use the afternoons for team planning, peer coaching, and reflection.

The primary question in evaluating the PDS pilot was to determine if this approach would improve the teaching performance of teacher candidates. This meant contrasting the performance of the PDS interns to the performance of teacher candidates in Towson's non-PDS Secondary program.

A comparison group was selected. The group included 10 social studies and English teacher candidates, who like the PDS group, were enrolled in discipline-specific methods courses and courses in their subject area major but not enrolled in the internship course. To verify that the PDS group and the comparison group were comparable on multiple measures, the two groups were compared in terms of grade point averages (GPA)—major, education, and overall. No significant differences were found on the GPA measures, thereby confirming that the selection process had not resulted in one group being academically superior to the other.

Both groups would have their first student teaching placement in a high school—the PDS group at Eastern Technical High School, the comparison group at various area high schools. Requests were made to the school systems involved to place at least one PDS and one comparison group student teacher in the same school for their middle school or second student teaching experience in order to control for location variables that might affect differences in teaching performance. An independent evaluator, not associated or familiar with the program, was hired to observe the PDS teacher candidates and the comparison teacher candidates. The evaluator was not privy to the purpose of assessing the PDS experience and did not know the identity of either the PDS or comparison group students.

Rubrics were written and field tested for the performance outcomes of classroom discipline, technology utilization, and reflection. A 4-point rating scale was used with 4 being exemplary, 3 being competent, 2 being marginally satisfactory, and 1 being unsatisfactory. Interview questions were developed to gather additional data about the experience of students from both groups. The evaluator was trained in the use of the rubrics and on the use of the interview questions to assure greater validity and reliability. The teacher candidates in both groups were informed through a letter from the department chair that they would be observed by an outside assessor as part of the program review process. The interns were observed and interviewed during the fourth or fifth week of their middle school (second) student teaching experience. Additionally, the university faculty member responsible for the pilot assessment collected qualitative data in the form of open-ended surveys and conducted structured interviews of teacher candidates, mentoring teachers, provisional teachers, school personnel, and university faculty.

1997—The Answer

There were positive results from the quantitative ratings of the independent assessor, demonstrating that the internship course, team-taught by university and high school faculty within the context of the real-world school environment, produced teacher candidates who were better prepared in three selected areas of teaching performance: (a) maintaining classroom discipline, (b) use of technology effectively for instruction, and (c) reflection on teaching (Neubert & Binko, 1998). The multivariate test of significance (Hotellings) revealed overall significance at the .007 level in favor of the PDS teacher candidates' performance. Qualitative data, based upon interviews and surveys of university and school professionals and students, confirmed that the PDS experience had a positive impact on the school. Respondents were nearly unanimous that it had enhanced the school curriculum and made relevant professional development opportunities available to school personnel. The high school staff members were particularly positive concerning the assistance with school improvement goals through intern participation in service projects as well as university faculty working together with school personnel on school improvement goals. The teacher candidates were judged by their mentor teachers at the PDS site as being more self-confident, more receptive to constructive criticism and reflection, and more realistic as to professional expectations than previous student teachers in the traditional student teaching program. Qualitative data based on self-reports by the teacher candidates revealed that they perceived themselves to be especially well prepared in classroom management, technology, and the ability to reflect. The cohort experience was found to be a successful security and growth factor for the interns as teachers.

Provisional teachers and their administrators were unanimous in their support of the Tuesday experience, especially having the time in a protected environment to discuss and reflect on their teaching. All eight of the provisional teachers in the PDS program were invited back to teach for the next academic year. The "powerful evidence" from this study (Teitel, 2000), particularly the statistically significant quantitative data on a relatively small number of subjects, revealed the positive impact of the PDS experience in addressing the needs of teacher candidates. In turn, faculty members in the Department of Secondary Education were supportive of the State PDS requirement. As a result, the faculty committed to expanding PDS internships to other high school and middle school sites in order to provide a professional development school opportunity to all secondary education teacher candidates.

1999—Another Question and Positive Answer

By 1999, the number of Towson University's secondary education PDS partnerships had expanded to an additional site in order to accommodate all students. A "site" became a partnership of a high school *and* a geographically proximate middle school, both of which were used for internships and student teaching experiences. A full-time PDS coordinator was hired to join the university faculty (the former site coordinator from Eastern Technical High School).

During a departmental faculty meeting, the question arose as to whether the PDS experience had *sustainable* effects for the graduates. A follow-up study was conducted with the purpose of determining if the differences noted in the performance of the participants in the professional development school had been sustained into the second year of classroom teaching.

Eight of the original PDS subjects and eight of the original comparison group members were located. They agreed to participate in "continuing program assessment" by being observed for one class period in the school to which they had been hired after graduation and then interviewed after the observation.

As in the original 1997 study, an independent evaluator was hired and trained in the use of the original rubrics and the interview questions. The assessor observed and interviewed the 16 subjects during a three-week period in January 1999. As with the observer in the initial study, the evaluator was "blind" to the purpose of the study, being told only that a program assessment was being conducted. Again, PDS and non-PDS subjects were not differentiated.

The multivariate test of significance (Hotellings) revealed overall significance at the .091 level for classroom discipline, use of technology, and reflection on teaching. Statistical analysis of the data revealed that the teachers trained in the PDS model demonstrated a tendency toward better performance in the areas of classroom discipline and the use of technology. The measure of the ability to reflect on their teaching was still significantly higher ($p<.01$) than those teachers who had not had the internship experience in a PDS (Neubert & Binko, 1999).

Status—2002

All secondary education students at Towson University now participate in a PDS program. There are five intern cohorts each academic year, five sites, five school site coordinators, and four university coordinators. Eastern Technical High School continues as a PDS site. The eight provisional teachers from Eastern are now certified and are still on the staff. The positive attitude toward PDS remains strong at Eastern. In fact, in 1999, after its Middle States Association evaluation and a Blue Ribbon School assessment and award, the principal proposed taking a hiatus from PDS involvement for a year to give the faculty a "breather," but the faculty voted unanimously to continue hosting the PDS.

The following characteristics currently define and guide the Secondary Education Professional Development School Program:

1. A PDS includes one middle and one high school.
2. Sites have a corps of master teachers who are willing to work as mentor teachers with English, social studies, science, math, special education, and foreign language interns.
3. The school faculty members from potential PDS sites engage with university faculty in an overview of the PDS model and a discussion of past research results after which time they vote on whether or not to become a PDS site.
4. Administrative leadership at the site school must support the adoption of the PDS model.
5. PDS sites need to be schools deemed "effective" according to state guidelines.
6. Each site must have at least one unique programmatic feature (e.g., inclusion, exceptional implementation of technology in the school, developmental reading across content areas, etc.).
7. A strategic planning workshop has to take place each Summer involving departmental faculty and site school faculty.
8. Each school working in a PDS partnership has a site coordinator selected from the faculty and awarded compensation in the form of assigned time or a stipend.
9. The department provides a faculty member who is the PDS coordinator/university liaison for each site.
10. The university coordinator conducts the internship course at the school one morning per week with the site coordinator and other partner school staff members.
11. The internship course continues to be offered in a teaching-hospital format.
12. Learning outcomes for the internship course have expanded and now consist of (a) classroom discipline, (b) reflection (including journals-intern peer coaching and portfolio development), (c) interactive instruction, and, (d) one other goal, selected at each individual site (e.g., literacy, critical thinking, use of technology, or inclusion.)

13. Reciprocity, even more now than in the past, is inherent in the PDS model. (For example, the university gives back to the school by having a faculty member serve on the school's site-based management team, providing a site-based graduate course, and having interns perform service learning projects.)

14. Quasi-experimental and qualitative evaluation continues to be conducted to determine the continued effectiveness of the model and to have data available to assist in making program enhancements and alterations as needed.

Note

1. The authors arc indebted to Mr. Robert Kemmery, Principal, and Mrs. Dorothy Hardin, Associate Principal, Eastern Technical High School, who began this PDS with us in 1996.

References

Maryland Higher Education Commission (1995). *Teacher education task force report*. Baltimore, MD: Author.

Neubert, G.A. & Binko, J.B. (1998). Professional development schools—The proof is in performance. *Educational Leadership*, *55*(5), 44–46.

Neubert, G. A. & Binko, J.B. (1999). Performance assessment of social studies and English teacher candidates trained in a secondary professional development school. Paper presented at the annual meeting of the American Educational Research Association, Montreal, Canada.

Stallings, J.A. (1991). Connecting pre-service teacher education and in-service professional development: A professional development school. Paper presented at the annual meeting of the American Association of Colleges for Teacher Education, Chicago. ERIC Document ED 339682.

Teitel, L. (1996). *Professional development schools: A literature review*. Washington, DC: National Council for the Accreditation of Teacher Education.

Teitel, L. (2000). What evidence exists for the effectiveness of professional development schools? Paper prepared for the National Council for Accreditation of Teacher Education, PDS Standards Field Test Project, Washington, DC. Education Department.

CHAPTER SIX

Conquering Boundaries: Collaborating Between Two Distinct Districts

Shelly S. Huggins & Todd Kenreich

Professional development school networks bring together multiple stakeholders to enhance teacher professional development and pre-service preparation (The Holmes Group, 1986; 1990). Guidance at the national (NCATE, 2001) and state level (Maryland State Department of Education, 1995) has helped many in Maryland make decisions about how to configure a PDS network. While the boundaries of a traditional PDS network do not extend across school districts (Walters, 1998), the work described in this chapter calls for regularly crossing district lines. As teacher-educators, we work with PDS partner schools in more than one school district.

One of the authors, Shelly, is an Elementary Education faculty member, and the other, Todd, is a member of the Towson faculty in Secondary Education. We work in separate programs with different PDS partner schools, but we have a shared experience of crossing school district boundaries. In this chapter, Shelly describes her work with an elementary PDS cohort that includes schools from two distinct districts. Maintaining a PDS cohort across two distinct districts offers many benefits and challenging opportunities for growth. Shelly provides a description of the origin of such collaboration and strategies to ease the management and transition process for all stakeholders. Todd describes his role in working with PDS partnerships in two school districts and explains the challenges associated with crossing boundaries.

Shelly: Cohort 3, How Did It Start?

Although there have been 27 PDS cohorts in Elementary Education, Cohort 3 is the only urban-based PDS site consisting of a site in a city school and one in a county school. A start-up grant was provided by the state higher education commission to establish an urban PDS. The two sites for Cohort 3 are unique, and the schools were selected to contrast with one another. The city site serves a 98% Caucasian community. The originators of Cohort 3 were enticed to consider the county site because of its unique demographic composition of being in a rural community serving a 98% African American population. The two schools are a perfect pairing to set interns' stereotypes upside down.

What Does It Look Like?

The semester before students begin their professional year, interns are permitted to indicate their preference of PDS locations. These preferences are given consideration, but the interns have no further input into their assigned placements. It is rare for interns to indicate Cohort 3 as their first choice. Once assigned, the interns often are intimidated by their assignment to complete part of their internship in a city school environment. Most often, students note concerns about their safety and their ability to handle aggressive classroom management issues as novice educators. At one point, an intern's parent called the PDS coordinator to determine who would be held accountable for any damage done to the intern's car if her child were forced to park it in "unsafe" areas of the city.

It is invigorating to have the same interns who dreaded the thought of entering the urban teaching environment come to care for and appreciate the learning communities they find. Many expand their priority areas for employment to include more urban areas after they have completed this urban experience. They have commented that they have seen some of the most committed and outstanding teachers in the city school. Several of them vie for and obtain positions at the city school after they graduate.

The interns in Cohort 3 rotate between the two districts in two placements. Their first placement in their professional year occurs during the Fall semester. After Christmas break, the interns return to their first placement for three weeks of full-time teaching and, then, switch to their second placement in the other district for the Spring semester.

So What? Benefits

One of the most promising aspects of participating in a cross-district PDS cohort is the many opportunities for "cross-pollination." Every PDS model provides for imbedded professional development opportunities that are exciting, but when the diverse aspects of two different districts are added, learning expands exponentially. During the interns' first placements, the PDS coordinator assures that imbedded professional development opportunities occur as new instructional techniques and technologies are shared with the interns, and they, in turn, bring them into their mentor teachers' classrooms.

Inevitably, the mentor teachers adopt some of the new strategies that interns use successfully. Upon adopting these new strategies, the mentor teachers make them their own, adapting them to the expectations of the district with their own pedagogical abilities, thus, adding a new and different twist to the interns' knowledge base. After the interns switch into their second placements and "pollinate" the new teaching environments with new strategies, the mentor teachers add individual flair and that district's expectations to each strategy. After these transformations, interns have a much more diverse bag of tricks for instructional planning and implementation. The evolution of pedagogical expertise is enhanced by the distinct educational environments created by the different districts.

The variety of professional development opportunities available to the interns in Cohort 3 due to access to both districts' professional development opportunities is an exciting aspect of "cross-pollination." It is especially interesting to have discussions with interns about how each district selects and maintains their professional development priorities and how resources are allocated. Interns are astute at recognizing the hidden and not-so-hidden agendas of each district. Being able to identify the differing cultures for each district seems to make the transition between their placements easier.

Interns in Cohort 3 are afforded the opportunity to see more diverse school organizational structures. They have opportunities for more involvement with diverse school-based administrators, central office personnel, and resource teachers, ultimately resulting in a more global understanding of how these stakeholders contribute to the learning community.

Opportunities for Growth

Engaging in the transition between the two placements in the two districts can be traumatic for many interns. The change in instructional expectations, time frames, and cultures is more dramatic when switching between districts and not just schools. The two districts require different lesson planning formats, different expectations for evaluating as well as displaying student work. The city district encourages teachers to wear a polo shirt that is identical to the student population's uniform, so even the interns' wardrobe requirements may drastically change.

Usually, the PDS coordinator can moderate the changes in expectations between districts. For example, the interns are allowed to follow any of the lesson planning formats of their teachers in each district. If the district is missing one of the ten components the PDS coordinator requires, the intern can simply add that aspect to the teacher's planning format. In the city district, teachers are required to display students' work around the classroom only if the rubric for assessing that work is concurrently displayed. In the county district, there are no such requirements for displaying students' work. In the city system, daily lesson plans are required to be on display and accessible in each classroom for the administration or other observers. The county system requires only the educational objective be evaluated and displayed daily.

Other differences between the districts are not as easily overcome. Different policies and procedures for each district make collaborations on projects difficult. For example, the preparation of interns in planning a field trip is much different between the districts. At the beginning of the semester, a member of the faculty from each district could easily work with the interns on how to negotiate these policies and complete the appropriate paperwork.

The governance of the PDS is often frustrating. For instance, providing meeting agendas and time frames at least two months in advance allows school personnel to determine the importance of their presence and input at these meeting and to seek someone else to represent them if they are not able to attend. It is rare to have all of the stakeholders attend each planning/collaborative meeting, making it a priority that clear and consistent communication of information occurs. Early in the school year, email distribution lists have to be developed, and they must be accurately maintained. The PDS coordinator has to have some "face time" contact with each stakeholder each week even when engaging in email communication.

The city PDS site is more than a 30-minute drive from the university and a 25-minute ride from the county PDS site. Often, this distance is compounded by heavy interstate traffic at key points, adding to the required commuting time period for the interns and the PDS coordinator. The interns are provided with detailed information about alternative routes from many directions to each school site. They are warned far in advance about tardiness and the practice of leaving early to beat the rush and arrive relaxed. However, a long commute is a challenging deterrent to cross-district collabora-tions. Meetings for interns are equally distributed to each school site so that no one group of interns has a longer commute than the others. The cost of the commute to the university in mileage reimbursement and wear and tear on the university PDS coordinator (and his or her car) is sizable. The university and the PDS coordinator lose productive hours sitting in traffic in the attempt to serve two different sites.

Ultimately, the many aspects of the cross-district collaboration are of benefit to the interns. Further, for the district, the quality of instruction of the interns and their participation at the schools far outweigh the challenges to the PDS organization.

Todd: My Secondary Experience

Unlike many teacher-educators, I first understood PDS from an intern's per-spective (see Miller, Ray, Dove, & Kenreich, 2000). This experience with PDS began as an intern in a Social Studies and Global Education PDS while a university student. After teaching social studies in a county school district in Maryland, I returned to my undergraduate university to pursue a doctoral degree in education. Part of my responsibilities as a doctoral student included work as a university supervisor of secondary social studies interns. As a su-pervisor, I quickly gained a deep understanding of the behind-the-scenes work that informs and sustains a PDS. Currently, I serve as a university liai-son for two PDSs in the Secondary Education program.

In another chapter of this book, my colleagues provide a more detailed account of the evolution of Towson's Secondary Education PDS program (see Chapter Five). Here I highlight experiences with two other Secondary PDS sites, both in adjoining districts. One of these PDS partnerships I helped to create, and the other was inherited. From this perspective, my "border-crossing" roles in working with two school districts' PDS sites are explored.

Two years ago my colleagues and I began talks with administrators of prospective partner schools in one of the county districts. The building ad-ministrators were eager to discuss the mutual benefits of becoming a PDS site. The selection of the high school and its feeder middle school stemmed in part from my interest in introducing interns to students with limited Eng-lish proficiency. The high school is an ESOL center for the eastern half of the county. As such, more than 20 languages are spoken by students. The ra-cial and ethnic composition of the student body is 27% African American,

1% American Indian, 9% Asian, 2% Hispanic, and 61% white. Nearly one in five students is eligible for free or reduced-price meals. The characteristics of this PDS make it an appealing site for introducing interns to diversity.

More recently, I assumed the role of liaison for a high school-middle school PDS in another county. The PDS I inherited is a mature yet vibrant partnership my university colleagues had nurtured for five years. The on-site coordinators provide solid leadership to the partnership. As a newcomer to this PDS, I arrived with a lot of questions about expectations for teachers, interns, and me. The site coordinators helped me see where expectations at this PDS converge with assumptions and experiences at my other PDS.

For example, in the Secondary Education PDS sites interns begin their Professional Year with a semester of a field-based course, "Internship in Secondary Education," followed by one semester of student teaching at the middle and high school. To assist with understanding about expectations at the first of the PDS partnerships I have described, members of the PDS Steering Committee and I designed the syllabus for the first semester of the Professional Year.

The school improvement plans of the partner schools inform the activities of each PDS. Service learning projects at both PDSs are designed to address specific objectives specified in the school improvement plans. During the first semester of the Professional Year, interns complete 30 hours of service projects at the high school and middle school. Many of these projects involve individual tutoring of ESOL students, and at-risk ninth graders and working with Saturday school students. Other service learning projects include engaging in parent outreach efforts and instructional technology initiatives. Aside from the benefits such work provides for interns, the service projects also help assure faculty, administrators, and parents that the PDS concretely enhances a school community.

It remains important to broadly frame a PDS as a site for teacher professional development and pre-service preparation. During summer strategic planning, I have to remind my colleagues of the need to prepare interns for success with student teaching and beyond. Sometimes, the interns choose to teach in central Maryland, but an increasing number seek teaching positions in New York, New Jersey, Florida, and California. Thus, care is taken to tailor the PDS experience so interns understand that expectations for teachers and students often vary considerably from school to school, district to district, and state to state.

Challenges

Coordinating two PDS partnerships in two school districts presents two central challenges: funding disparities and building a shared discourse. Since its inception, the PDS movement has wrestled with issues associated with funding (Clark & Plecki, 1997). In one school district, funding priorities allow for greater support of PDS site coordinators through assigned time and modest stipends. The district also pays teachers for their attendance at PDS Summer planning meetings. In the other district, PDS site coordinators receive modest stipends, but there is no assigned time. The district is reluctant to pay teachers for their time with PDS Summer planning. In working with both districts, news about funding disparities travels quickly among stakeholders. In the end, the university must be poised, or perhaps forced, to address these inequities. In an era of budget shortfalls, a public university has to carefully calculate its own ability to support PDS activities.

Beyond money, language presents a persistent challenge. Although Maryland recently circulated a much-needed glossary of PDS terms (Maryland Partnership for Teaching and Learning K–16, 2003), stakeholders in various settings employ terms differently. For example my title is IHE Liaison: "[this is] the point person for the IHE in the PDS partnership" (p. 35). Yet, in one PDS, my title is "university coordinator," and at the other my title is "PDS Liaison." Perhaps the lack of a uniform language for talking about PDS reflects the organic nature of PDS partnerships. Local stakeholders position the "official" language of PDS within their own discourses. Some teachers resist terms such as "internship" for the more familiar term of "student teaching." Over time, the language of PDS will become more settled. For now, it is important to talk with stakeholders about key terms so that our communication is clear. With a shared language, there will be a better understanding of aims, activities, and roles within a PDS.

A Next Step

In both school districts considerable pressure exists for increased student achievement as measured by multiple assessments at the district, state, and national level. In the midst of the calls for high-stakes assessment, mentors urge interns not to reduce teaching and learning in favor of constant test preparation. While test-taking skills are important, education should prepare individuals for civic participation in a global society. To that end, my colleagues and I at the university are working to promote cross-cultural learning within PDS sites. There are robust opportunities for cross-cultural exchanges: email exchanges between teachers, students, and interns in different countries, study abroad opportunities for P–12 faculty and administrators, and, PDS site visits for teachers, administrators, and teacher-educators from abroad. All of us look forward to taking the idea of boundary crossing to a new level.

References

Clark, R.W., & Plecki, M.L. (1997). Professional development schools: Their costs and financing. In M. Levine & R. Trachtman (Eds.), *Making professional development schools work: Politics, practice, and policy* (pp. 134–158). New York: Teachers College Press.

Holmes Group (1986). *Tomorrow's teachers: A report of The Holmes Group.* East Lansing, MI: Author.

Holmes Group (1990). *Tomorrow's schools: Principles for the design of professional development schools.* East Lansing, MI: Author.

Maryland Partnership for Teaching and Learning K–16 (2003). Professional development schools: An implementation manual. Baltimore: Maryland State Department of Education.

Maryland State Department of Education, Professional Development School Consortium (1995). *Common understandings about professional development schools.* Baltimore: Author.

Miller, S. L, Ray, S., Dove, T., & Kenreich, T. (2000). Perspectives on personal professional development. In M. Johnston, P. Brosnan, D. Cramer & T. Dove (Eds.), *Collaborative reform and other improbable dreams: The challenges of professional development schools* (pp. 141–151). Albany: SUNY Press.

National Council for the Accreditation of Teacher Education (2001). *Standards for professional development schools.* Washington, DC: Author.

Walters, S. (1998). Walking the fault line: Boundary spanning in professional development schools. *Teaching and Change, 6,* 90–106.

PART THREE

Transforming Teacher Preparation and Professional Development

Connecting Teacher Preparation and Continuing Professional Development: The Boundary Spanner's Role

Pamela W. Morgan & Ann M. Eustis

Introduction

To know one's past is not to live in the past or to be stymied in the present. The past contains seeds to the future.

Dr. Asa G. Hilliard, III (1995)

Connecting teacher preparation and continuing professional development is a critical function of any PDS partnership but one that cannot be discussed with any degree of accuracy without revisiting the events of the past that produced "the seeds" for the present. After understanding that workable linkages between ongoing professional development and teacher preparation existed, the boundary spanner role, geared toward facilitating linkages that address this learning continuum, was created. Over time the boundary spanner has been known as the instructional facilitator for the PDS and presently, the PDS site coordinator. The distinction in titles reflects partnership agreements with a particular school district.

As defined by Berry & Catoe (1994), "boundary spanners [are] individuals who are accepted in all institutions." Ideally, individuals who serve effectively as boundary spanners must have instant credibility in each of the institutions (the university and the school) they represent. However, measures of credibility vary within institutions and with individuals within those institutions. Time and experience are instrumental in bridging the credibility expectations for the institutions within the partnership.

A PDS must be a dynamic entity—always in a state of becoming. The boundary spanner's role is one that has fluctuated and must continue to do so. As faculty members in the University's Elementary Education department and as practitioners in local Baltimore Metropolitan Area school districts, we have experienced firsthand what Teitel, Reed & O'Connor (1998) would consider to be a key component of sustainability in a PDS—creating a critical mass of players who can comfortably live in the intersection of what had traditionally been non-permeable worlds, that of the institution of higher education and of the local education agency.

In the discussions that follow, we will recount our respective experiences as boundary spanners in the same university but in two different school systems during different eras in the history of this partnership. In the process, successes and challenges associated with building a new third culture rather than merging two existing cultures will be shared.

Pamela's Experiences: 1995–2000

In the Beginning...

The Department of Elementary Education was one of the first departments in the College of Education to participate in the university's PDS initiative when two members of the department began their groundbreaking work with the first PDS cohort of interns at an elementary school in Baltimore County. At the time, 1994, the PDS effort was being coordinated by a full-time Elementary Education faculty member. When that faculty member accepted a position with another university in the summer of 1995, it was decided to fill the position by creating two positions to be jointly funded by the university and Baltimore County Public Schools (BCPS).

An agreement was reached to establish the boundary-spanning position of "instructional facilitator for professional development schools." Thus, the responsibility for coordinating the PDS became the priority for two educators instead of one. The creative funding structure for these positions meant that for personnel and payroll purposes these individuals would technically be employees of the county school district, with the school system paying one half of the salary. The other half was paid by the University through a grant arrangement although no "soft" money was involved. The individuals who would fill those positions would devote 50% of their time as regular Elementary Education faculty teaching two courses for the department. During the other 50% of those individuals' time, they would work as staff members in the county's Office of Staff Development, housed on the university campus.

While reading *The Baltimore Sun* one Sunday in early August 1995, I came across a position announcement that was distinguished by the university logo. The announcement described the newly created position of instructional facilitator for professional development schools, listed the requirements and responsibilities for the position, and specified the application process and deadline. This job description has since affectionately been dubbed the "walk on water" version. Although I knew nothing about the PDS (I can admit that now), the responsibilities sounded like something that I would be interested in doing, especially because I had a newly earned master's degree in leadership in teaching, a 2-year-old Milken Family Foundation National Educator Award, and an evolving passion for working with pre-service teachers sparked by years of coordinating student teaching and other types of placements for my school, mainly for the university's students. Surely I could perform this job and learn about PDS in the process, so I applied.

Subsequently, I interviewed for the position and was offered the position. My tenure as an instructional facilitator for the PDS began in September of 1995. This excerpt from my PDS journal captures my mixed emotions quite profoundly:

> Today was my first day in my new position. I met with [the Elementary Education Department Chair] in the morning at TSU to get departmental information and learned that my colleague will not be joining me because she was waiting to be released by her principal who was seeking a suitable replacement. I met with [the personnel director] in the afternoon at Greenwood to discuss my contract. He admitted to being embarrassed to learn that my base salary actually constituted a pay cut for me and imagine my surprise when I discovered the discrepancy after being told in the interview that I would probably get a pay raise. (What a leap! I don't believe I actually resigned from my tenured position with Baltimore city before I actually got a written commitment from Baltimore county. What's happening to me? I can't recall ever taking such a risk; either I must be slipping or I must be really intrigued by this work).

After 22 years as a public school educator and eight of them as a language arts department head, I was ready for a change, not because I was unhappy with where I was or what I was doing, rather because I was ready for a new challenge. The old adage, "Be careful what you ask for; you just may get it" is appropriate for what was about to unfold.

Bridging Two Cultures

A major expectation was that of bridging the two cultures, the public school and the university, to create a collaborative relationship in which the PDS would thrive. There were so many challenges to face and hurdles to clear before we could get on with culture bridging. While both of us were respected practitioners with demonstrated expertise in public education, one complication for me was I needed to learn the cultures of two new institutions simultaneously and alone since it would not be until 1996 that my colleague would start her work. Fortunately, I was allowed to "shadow" an Elementary Education faculty member for that first semester so I could get a feel for how things worked in higher education. Other faculty members allowed me to sit in on their classes as well.

Like a loyal ethnographer, I spent the initial weeks in my new position talking to colleagues, visiting pilot schools, and talking to P–12 educators about the Elementary Education PDS initiative. I heard story upon story about how the initiative came to be. The gist of the stories was that the PDS was a top-down effort, and the residual effects were quite evident in the limited number of full-time faculty actively involved in PDS work, not to mention the range in attitudes and emotions that accompanied these accounts. After what seemed like an eternity of listening to such stories, my focus changed from examining the history to contemplating what happens next. The question that I began posing to colleagues was framed something like, "I understand the history, but if PDS is mandated in the *Redesign of Teacher Education in Maryland*, where do we go from here?"

One of the major turning points in the department's and the college's PDS efforts came about with the naming of a new department chair and creation of a PDS steering committee affording the department a relatively organized space to discuss PDS issues. This discussion has evolved with time in the focus and tone of the exchange. Consequently, though, the business of culture bridging was being shared, but progress was still minimal.

It was not until I attended the Louisville National PDS Conference in Spring 1996 with a group of P–16 educators from the partnership that the culture-bridging issue was clarified. As the other PDS instructional facilitator and I listened to Deborah Meier deliver her keynote address, we both had an "aha" experience. As though she were talking directly to us, she proclaimed, "Don't waste your time trying to bridge two cultures; simply build a new one!" Finally, the answer to the dilemma. We had figured out through trial and error that the overriding challenge of trying to bridge the cultures is dealing with the reality of non-negotiable structures with inflexible schedules, different mandates for student performance, and protocols sometimes better understood rather than being made explicit. Meier's advice about creating a new culture moved us on a more productive odyssey.

The Third Culture

The partnership continued to promote shared governance by maintaining a PDS coordinating council, a governing body of P–16 representation that convened monthly to evaluate and determine partnership actions, activities, and fiscal matters. To facilitate communication among the partners, we designed and published a partnership newsletter that became known as "PDS Today." Because grant funds were prevalent at the time, a number of proposals were written; thus, the partnerships were strengthened by providing for the professional development needs of pre- and in-service educators, a feature of PDS that distinguishes it from practices in traditional teacher preparation programs. Also, professional development opportunities were organized for practicing educators that were open to pre-service educators. These opportunities took the form of institutes—Summer, back-to-school, Winter, and Springtime—addressing the partnership slogan: "A Community of Learners: Building Best Practices." The topics included minority student achievement, performance-based assessment and instruction, multiple intelligences, and teacher research. Local and national presentations by PDS partners were made about our efforts with presenters reflecting the P–16 partnership. Often, interns were included as presenters. Numerous graduate courses were offered exclusively for professional educators that convened off-campus at PDS sites and at significantly reduced out-of-pocket costs to the educators. In doing so, a track record was established, laying the foundation for the Towson Learning Network (TLN) to represent one of the university's successful efforts at institutionalizing PDS by providing professional development opportunities in the schools.

Challenges

Initially, fulfilling the district half of the instructional facilitator position was interpreted as working directly in the three pilot schools; however, the university time line for staffing courses required schedules to be drafted at least a semester in advance, so teaching two courses for the students assigned to those schools was not always possible. Consequently, I had to teach two courses in the traditional program while working with teachers in two of the three schools as well as serving on their school improvement teams to fulfill P–12 responsibilities. As the district leadership changed, so did job expectations.

By the Summer of 1999, the name of the district Office of Staff Development had been changed to "The Department of Professional Development." The number of personnel devoted to PDS efforts had gone from 3 to 2 to 1—me! Deliberate efforts were made to involve me in systemwide initiatives including designing and delivering presentations for the district's new hires at new teacher induction, for mentor teachers, for members of school improvement teams, and for the achievement facilitators. By my last year in the position, I coordinated all of the PDS partnerships in the district. This meant I was interacting with representatives from 13 different institutions of higher education during 2.5 days a week while managing two PDS grants and performing other duties associated with being a member of the Department of Professional Development. This challenge resulted in my establishing the district PDS consortium that was proposed in the previous year's PDS continuation grant.

As mentioned, there were complications in assuming the instructional facilitator role revolving around the need to learn about two new institutional cultures. Another complication was a more subtle, implicit, though major one—confronting daily my position as a minority by virtue of my acceptance of the instructional facilitator position. While this may seem like an odd statement to make, one must understand that although my race and ethnicity classify me as a minority in the larger society, I had actually enjoyed majority status in most of the circles in which I traveled. With the exception of my high school years, the only other times that I tended to be in the minority were during encounters as a teacher-consultant with the Maryland Writing Project and as a teacher-researcher in a National Writing Project program.

I embarked upon this new professional journey quite confident in my ability to interact in this new diverse environment. However, the effects of the culture shock proved to be more overwhelming than I could have understood beforehand. I never envisioned myself becoming a civil rights activist, not in 1995, but often found myself having to be the face and voice of diversity everywhere I went, having to battle issues of equity and diversity for myself, for non-tenured teachers, and for the university's students. This left me feeling burned out from having to serve on numerous search committees so that these efforts met university diversity standards. As impressive as I believed my credentials to be, particularly in the P–12 arena, there were times I felt my credibility was suspect because I was operating in a new environment and because of my packaging. There was considerable extra effort in time and energy so that I could establish credibility in ways that colleagues who did not look like me ever had to contemplate or experience. Since being invisible has never been a viable option for me, I had to adjust quickly if I were to be an effective change agent.

The Change Agent's Lens

According to Rogers, "The change agent is an individual who influences clients' innovation-decisions in a direction deemed desirable by a change agency. Consequently, change agents act as linkers between the change agency and clients." (Rogers, 1995, p. 27) This description accurately captures the essence of the boundary spanner role of instructional facilitator for professional development schools. As such I was expected to link the cultures and engage them in effectively adopting the targeted innovation. When Rogers talks about innovation, he is referring to technology almost exclusively. For the purposes of this discussion, my frame of reference in using innovation is in terms of the PDS initiative. Our university experienced significant change that was imposed by external forces, and that factor resulted in a somewhat messy process characterized by the challenges revealed in the previous discussion.

Consistent with Rogers's theory of diffusion of innovation, the PDS partnership consists of all the categories of adopters. There are innovators (those adventurous people who constitute the first 5% of adopters), early adopters (the local, respected risk-takers who represent the next 10% of adopters), the early majority (those who interact quite a bit with their peers, deliberate for a significant period of time prior to deciding to become adopters and represent the next 35%), the late majority (the following 35% who become adopters when resistance is no longer a safe tactic), and laggards (the final 15% who may or may not become adopters).

The PDS and the boundary spanners have come quite a distance in a brief period of time. There is quite a distance to go due to the extensive and intensive nature of PDS work. One of the first slogans that we adopted came from a "Dilbert" comic strip that read, "Change is good; you go first." Courtesy of one of our former partner schools, the revised draft of that quote became "Change is good; we'll go first." The fact the university has earned local and national recognition for its PDS efforts is evidence that we have gone first.

Successes

The creation of the third culture has resulted in numerous successes in the partnership including but not limited to those to be discussed here. First, we no longer have to make the distinction of having a traditional program and a PDS program since the traditional Elementary Education program and PDS are now synonymous. Due to the labor intensity associated with PDS efforts, more full-time faculty are now involved in PDS. This increase in faculty involvement comes as a result of demand driven supply. In Fall 1997, my cohort of PDS interns complained about being a cohort because it placed additional demands on their time as well as other resources required to meet heightened performance expectations. By Fall 2000, however, the interns were complaining about substandard preparation because they were *not* in a PDS. After semesters of fearing there would be not enough placements for the interns, now there are more teachers expressing interest in being mentors than there are interns to place. This occurred because teachers split an internship rotation, instead of one teacher hosting two interns in a given semester, the mentor serves as a host to one intern, thus allowing another colleague to have the same opportunity. The interns feel quite positive, knowing teachers want to share their space with them in contrast to being with a teacher who has been coerced into mentoring an intern.

Many successes have come about due to missteps. It was discovered that clear articulation is necessary for establishing additional PDS sites after the embarrassment of having to curtail involvement in one of the original pilot schools because of a district's administrator's concern regarding the high percentage of non-tenured teachers and the school's need for a mentor for those teachers. Thus, more effective collaboration with the appropriate P–12 partnership representative(s) is needed to identify acceptable schools for forming future partnerships.

PDS work is labor intensive for university faculty and for P–12 faculty. Therefore, school partners need to take time off due to staff turnover and/or feelings of burnout. This means establishing levels of PDS involvement that allow a P–12 partner to remain in the partnership availing itself of professional development opportunities while the school is on hiatus in hosting and mentoring interns.

There have been shifts in colleagues' attitudes about the instructional facilitator position from that of suspicion to that of acceptance to that of publicly admitting, *"we need more Pams."* The quote appearing in the University-County Professional Development School internal evaluation report (Maxwell, Morgan, & Proffitt, 1999) says it all: *"The Instructional Facilitator position is a critical feature that has influenced change by substantive linkage of the university and public school—fulfills boundary spanning role."*

Ironically, as my tenure as instructional facilitator for the PDS was ending, Ann's was just beginning. Due to budgetary constraints, the position on which Ann's was modeled was eliminated by the system that had pioneered it and inspired other institutions to create similar roles. Ann and I had the opportunity to exchange ideas about the role over lunch. We discussed the benefits and the pitfalls as well as the gray areas I learned were inherent in a joint position. Thus, Ann was able to approach her new role as PDS site coordinator with far less apprehension than she would have had her position not been informed by my experiences.

Ann's Experiences: 2000–2003

The *Standards for Maryland Professional Development Schools* were being field tested and refined at the same time the Ellicott City, Maryland, partnership was "becoming." Thus, there was clear focus on the partnership's organization, on the specific roles of various stakeholders, and on how resources were used. This, along with the pioneering work Pamela had done during the early years of the partnership as an instructional facilitator, was, in my view, the primary reason I was somewhat successful in the role of PDS site coordinator for this PDS. My experiences in the jointly appointed position began in the Summer of 2000 and extended through the Summer of 2003 in a multi-site PDS in a suburban school district.

According to the *Standards for Maryland Professional Development Schools*, (2001),

> PDS partners allocate resources to support the continuous improvement of teaching and learning. New roles are created and old roles are modified for PreK–16 students, interns, faculty, and administrators to achieve the mission of the PDS. Effective communication about PDS plans and structures plays a key role in the

linkage with school districts, IHEs, parents, and others. Jointly funded positions are encouraged and supported. Partners provide PDS stakeholders with necessary resources to advance PDS work: vision, time, space, incentives, leadership, technology, and access (pp. 7–8)

The PDS in which I worked was developed in the Winter and Spring of 2000 as the Elementary Education Program needed new sites, and this county district wanted to transform some of its teacher center sites into PDS partnerships. As memoranda were being drafted, the idea of a jointly funded program coordinator was discussed. Since I was on leave from a district elementary classroom to instruct at the University and had previous experiences with the PDS at other institutions of higher education, I lobbied my department chair, deans, and the county PDS coordinator to be considered for the boundary spanner role. The appointment was a career goal of mine. The appointment was made and greeted warmly in the county, where I was a "known" in the PDS movement and had been successful in the elementary classroom.

The partnership the university formed with the county adopted a two-tiered governance structure with a Management Team (comprised of the county PDS coordinator, the university's department chair, building administrators, and myself) as well as a larger, diverse Steering Committee (comprised of the aforementioned personnel and others including interns, special educators, and parents). These groups met monthly with the management team adopting the agenda for the steering committee. Decisions were made by the Steering Committee on a consensus basis. Individuals who served on the committee became or were site-based leaders and vocal PDS proponents. A position was adopted in each school site known as the site liaison. These leaders were identified by the building administrators and served for a year at a time, receiving compensation. Having these "first responders" at each site was a necessity as they could serve as the "go to" persons when I was not there, and they could help facilitate effective communication about programs and mediate concerns.

The role that I filled was delineated over time as the point person for the university in the particular partnership and as the empowered representative of the school sites, providing leadership to the PDS. Because the role evolved over time, it was not until just before I left that I was able to specify for the first time detailed job functions that could be used to advertise for a replacement. The essential job functions were:

- teaching and supervising the equivalent of two courses each semester
- perform the duties of a university PDS supervisor
- provide on-site coordination and facilitate communication among university staff, building administrators, and teachers
- make internship placements in collaboration with building administrators
- co-plan and implement programs for interns, mentors, and staff
- assist and support professional development opportunities for county and university staff
- co-plan and facilitate steering committee and other governance meetings
- assist with partnership-building activities
- assist with budgetary and financial management specifics
- serve as a member of a countywide PDS coordinating committee
- serve as a member of the university's Department of Elementary Education
- assist in collecting documentation for program evaluation purposes
- serve as a liaison to the district's Office of Human Resources
- promote PDS initiatives and training countywide.[1]

Resources in this partnership were readily available during its first three years (my tenure) of this position. Title II monies and support from the district were used to support PDS work. Half of a teaching position (salary and benefits) provided the district's one-half of the position while the University supported the other half. The district also provided funding for site liaison stipends, supplies and material costs, and workshops for professional development activities such as mentor training. These expenses were part of the district's annual budget. In addition, each year building administrators made sure there was designated space for the PDS program. This included classroom space to hold intern courses on site and office space for me. This abundance had a positive impact on the service I performed in this position.

In reflecting on the entirety of my experience, Pamela's experiences and advice allowed me to avoid pitfalls right from the start as the PDS was forming. For instance, those in the district and at the university to whom I reported never required or wanted an accounting of how my time was spent. I had the freedom to structure and organize my time as long as I posted contact information at my various sites. [Note: I do remember one of the building administrators asking me early on to whom I reported. I did not take this as evidence that he thought I was a slacker, but only that I was on the payroll for his school and he wanted to make sure he was not supposed to be evaluating me. I assured him this was a technicality because I was a "release teacher" and that I had to be assigned somewhere, so only on paper was I officially part of his faculty.] Over time, my weekly schedule became more regular, and it was maintained for the most part during the three years. Mondays were for countywide meetings and college meetings. Tuesdays through Thursdays were field based for teaching courses and providing supervision. Fridays, ideally, were for doing administrative work or working with administrative assistants at either the university or the district PDS office.

At the university and in Maryland school districts, there is a cadre of people known as "PDSers." This group expands each year as the PDS becomes more institutionalized and it becomes evident the PDS far exceeds the old teacher center model. At the university, more and more faculty are involved in PDS work in some capacity. Thus, there was a new "third culture" of joint work at the university and in the schools.

There soon became a critical mass of those faculty members participating in this third culture. We were able to achieve this "critical mass," considered an essential element of PDS sustainability (Teitel et al., 1998), in part, because of the credibility of the boundary spanner role. Since I had been involved in professional development schools as a mentor and adjunct instructor, while involved full time as an elementary classroom teacher in the county for many years, the credibility I established was important. As I was keenly aware that the concept of a university partnership where power and decision-making were shared was a foreign one to school people, it helped that I had been where they now were.

For example, there was disbelief and some rebellion when mentor teachers in the school realized their input was critical in developing the scope of the undergraduate internship. The same was true when their feedback was sought for such matters as integrating the interns' course assignments with the Elementary Education curriculum and deciding what graduate courses and continuing professional development workshops they themselves needed. The mentors were used to being told what to do. It was a radical shift for them to have a program director need, request, and value their input. In this role, I learned the importance of developing trust and having rapport with mentors and other site-based leaders. Even though there were myriad situations where it would have been easier to dictate decisions, I made sure we governed by consensus. In doing so, I would speak from my own prior experiences and present ideas used by other university partnerships. Then, it would be up to all of us to develop initiatives and requirements. When I could effectively communicate the benefits of program requirements to the mentors (and other site-based leaders), it was easy to achieve "buy-in" and increase the ranks of "PDSers "

During my three-year experience, I worked hard to identify and develop site-based leaders. This helped with the implementation of the PDS model because the requirements of the site coordinator were difficult for one person to achieve. It was never meant to be "my" PDS. As the PDS evolved, delegating tasks became easier and easier. More site-based personnel embraced the program as "theirs." As I anticipated ending my time in the joint role, I felt compelled to lobby that the position would still exist beyond my tenure. Part of the strength of the PDS model is for boundary spanners to grow and develop. There is a new site coordinator serving in the boundary spanner role. For the time being, there remains a commitment on the part of the university and the county to continue to co-fund the position.

Final Thoughts

Serving as a boundary spanner has been a life-changing experience for the two of us, as our discussions indicate. We faced challenges and learned a lot. Among the conclusions that can be drawn from our collective experiences is whether or not the notion of a boundary spanner as it is currently conceived and implemented is feasible.

Given the differences in the two cultures of the public schools and higher education, the concept and practice of academic freedom make the boundary-spanning position more conducive to higher education culture than to public school culture. Merely acknowledging this "reality," though, defeats the nature and purpose of the position. Public school culture tends to seek to control professionals by placing them in a hierarchical structure. The university, in contrast, has a different culture with more freedom and less control and a different system of advancement to tenure and promotion.

If the true nature of collaboration of the position of instructional facilitator/PDS site coordinator is to be realized, the third culture must be allowed to evolve into one in which professionals are respected and treated as such because their integrity and preparation combine to create the ultimate driving force of accountability. This would be a significant and welcomed change.

One labor negotiations study offers support for further reconceptualizing boundary spanning with the finding that "boundary spanning is a differentiated function that is not necessarily loaded on to one person" but in the collective efforts of the organization or partnership (Friedman & Pololny, 1992, p. 18). From the successes shared in our work, we can infer that extending the scope of the boundary-spanning concept will foster the sustainability of the PDS partnership. The increased active involvement of full-time faculty in PDS work is a great step in that direction.

We end this discussion of our boundary-spanning experiences with an acknowledgment and a challenge. The acknowledgment is that "People don't resist change; they resist being changed" (Sparks, 1997, Par. 3). The challenge is as follows:

> There will no doubt be numerous areas where we make a difference—within ourselves, our families, our profession. It takes no effort to complain about what's wrong; it takes dedication and tenacity to get in there and change things...we are as strong as we allow ourselves to be. We have as much influence as we permit ourselves. Whether we act on our own or need to gather forces in order to shake things up, the power rests with us (Copage, 1995).

Note

1. Adapted from Howard County Public School System position vacancy announcement, June 2003.

References

Berry, B., & Catoe, S. (1994). Creating professional development schools. In L. Darling-Hammond (Ed.), *Professional development schools: Schools for developing a profession* (pp. 176–202). New York: Teachers College Press.

Copage, E. (1995). *Black pearls for parents.* New York: William Morrow & Company.

Friedman, R.A. & Podolny, J. (1992). Differentiation of boundary spanning roles: Labor negotiations and implications for role conflict. *Administrative Science Quarterly, 37,* 28–47.

Hilliard, A. (1995). *The maroon within us.* Baltimore: Black Classic Press.

Maryland Partnership for Teaching and Learning K-16 Superintendents and Deans Committee (2003). *Professional development schools:An implementation manual.* Baltimore: Maryland State Department of Education.

Maxwell, D., Morgan, P. W., & Proffitt, T. (1999). An internal evaluation report: The Towson University-Baltimore County Public Schools Professional Development School Network. Towson, MD: Towson University, College of Education.

Maryland State Department of Education (2001). *Standards and guidelines for professional development schools in Maryland.* Baltimore, MD: Author.

Rogers, E. (1995). *Diffusion of innovations.* New York: The Free Press.

Sparks, D. (1997, March). Is resistance to change really the problem? *The Developer.* Retrieved October 24, 2003, from http://www.msdc.org/library/developer/dev3-97sparks.html.

Teitel, L., Reed, C. & O'Connor, K. (1998). Institutionalizing professional development schools: Successes, challenging, and continuing tensions. In Nancy Lauter (Ed.) *Professional development schools: Confronting realities.* New York: National Center for Restructuring Education, Schools, and Teaching, 1–63.

CHAPTER EIGHT

Transforming Faculty Roles by Waving the Magic Wand

Gregory Bryant, Nechie Rochel King,
Jane E. Neapolitan, Maggie Madden,
& Lauren Rifkin

In the *Redesign of Teacher Education in Maryland* (1995) Maryland teacher education institutions are required to create PDSs for the preparation of teacher candidates. The PDS model is an attempt to change the traditional, cooperative relationship between K–12 school systems and institutions of higher education to a collaborative, transformational relationship. As traditional roles become blurred, the expectation is these two distinct cultures will blend somehow. This naïve idea has appeared in the teacher education literature and in job descriptions of faculty from both cultures simultaneously exposing a deep divide between the traditional roles of P–12 teachers and higher education faculty.

As more PDS partnerships are developed, higher education faculty are being "ask[ed] to let go of important beliefs, significant allegiances, and deeply ingrained practices" (Trachtman, 1997, p. 190). Faculty members must continuously reinvent themselves as they go about their work with school-based partners and attempt to influence whole-school reform (Holmes Group, 1995). Formal preparation for taking on this new transformative role, though, is virtually absent in the higher education community. Mentoring for doing PDS work is scarce. Further, PDS work often does not coincide with more traditional expectations for faculty members' performance in teaching, scholarship, and service. Even in institutions where PDS work is part of the promotion and tenure process, higher education faculty sacrifice reflection, analysis, and the collegial nature of the academy over the demands of having to take action (Teitel, 2001). Thus, there is a need for faculty to engage in reflective practice about PDS initiatives and to share their learning with others involved with and/or interested in PDS work. Without essential reflection and analysis, the external pressures on the work of higher education faculty will continue to intensify as is the case for classroom teachers, school administrators, and teacher-educators in general (Apple, 2001).

Developing a PDS is more akin to waving a magic wand, then, in pulling the rabbit out of a hat, except the magician usually can predict the outcome of the attempt. In this case, most faculties have had difficulty visualizing outcomes. Would we prepare better teachers? Would we learn to work together? What is a hybrid faculty member? How would each group survive in the other's world? Is there any person who is an insider in both cultures? Questions, questions, and more questions produced very few signs of the rabbit. A great deal of wand waving, however, eventually has led to a range of outcomes from anxiety and burnout to a sense of success in both worlds.

Four stories make up this chapter. The first is "While the theory is powerful, the practice is often overwhelming and exhausting." The next is "Transforming the veteran into a PDS advocate", while the third is "The university PDS liaison as a resistant immigrant." The fourth is "PDS as a catalyst for change."

The authors of these sections include three Towson faculty members (Jane, Greg, Nechie), and a fourth (Lauren) is from a Towson PDS partnership school. They have extensive experiences in the transformation from university faculty to PDS liaisons and coordinators within the Towson University Professional Development School Network. Their stories are an examination of how university faculty are challenged and transformed into a new version of a teacher-educator—one who becomes immersed in the culture of the schools yet at the same time examines biases and allegiances to the past and to the campus. The fourth story is about the transition from a traditional role as a classroom teacher to a mentor and university adjunct faculty member. There is a concluding narrative (Maggie) from a PDS Network Coordinator at the Maryland State Department of Education.

Jane: "While the Theory Is Powerful, the Practice Is Often Overwhelming and Exhausting"

Let me preface my story by saying, the PDS movement has been very good to me. During the past four years, I have worked as a PDS researcher, mentor, and collaborator. I am a faculty member at a university deeply committed to the PDS movement. Like my colleagues, I have taken up the challenge of serving as a university liaison and working with teacher candidates and their mentor teachers. Much of my work has been framed by the new PDS standards of the National Council for the Accreditation of Teacher Education (NCATE) and the State of Maryland. In 2001, the Dean of the College of Education gave me the charge to create the Institute for Professional Development School Studies at Towson University. The institute is a research and development initiative to celebrate the history and accomplishments of the Towson PDS network (including this book), educates the community about the processes and products of PDS activity, and collaboratively conducts improvement-oriented inquiry that contributes to whole-school reform. Through these various experiences, I have found that doing PDS work in a deep and transformative way is not for the faint hearted. A PDS is not a place for a prima donna who might pass through a schoolhouse without establishing relationships, building trust, and looking at one's practice honestly.

In this section, I share the story of being transformed from an "outsider" to an "insider" in a professional development school. The indicator I use for becoming an insider is *if and when I am consulted on important decisions in the partnership.* Consulting with the university PDS liaison on any issue denotes a change from a cooperative (traditional) to a collaborative (transformational) approach to leadership in the new counterculture. The basis for this story is a reflection journal I have kept during my time as a university PDS liaison. The names of friends and colleagues have been changed to ensure confidentiality.

On the Outside, Wanting to Get in

While a new faculty member at my university in 1999, I was asked to serve as the research liaison for the NCATE PDS Standards Field Test Project involving one of our PDS partnerships. In this role, I would be supervising teacher candidates at the PDS and collecting data for an inquiry project in which the focus was on performance-based assessment examining the impacts of working with performance assessment on teacher candidates, mentor teachers, and children (Neapolitan & Harper, 2001). Having the chance to carry out a microethnographic study in a PDS (with funding to support it, no less!) was a dream come true for a qualitative researcher. My wish list for transcription costs, qualitative data analysis software, a graduate research assistant, and course release time had all been granted.

Little did I know that coming into the PDS in the middle of the year as an outsider would bring complications. I had *assumed* the mentor teachers would jump at the chance to participate with me and the teacher candidates in a research project!

"Judith," my researcher friend, said she would be a support. I wrote to her:

> I wondered if any of the other sites were having difficulty getting their mentor teachers to participate in their inquiry projects? As of last week, I had only three out of 15 mentors give their consent. Apparently, most of them objected to writing a one-page weekly reflection on their teaching. Same old excuse of "not having enough time" was given. I went back to them and said, one paragraph, if that would make it better. I have not checked yet to see if any more have agreed to participate.
>
> Because I'm new at [the PDS], I realize that I haven't had a chance to establish "trust and rapport" with the mentors yet. I also have a hunch that this new focus on THEIR teaching (and by a newcomer, no less) is making them uneasy. Your suggestions or comments on this would be appreciated. (March 6, 2000).

Judith wrote back:

> It seems to me that you and your colleagues are experiencing some of the "challenges" associated with conducting inquiry. It takes awhile for practitioners to agree to collect information. And then it might take even longer for them to use the results of their data collections and analysis. My guess is that this activity becomes especially tricky when participants feel as though the decision to "collect information" about a new initiative is not part of the initial agreement to try something new. At your PDS, mentors may feel as though your request related to this inquiry represents additional work that was not part of their Summer Institute planning process.
>
> It may be prudent to scale back your inquiry and focus on the ways in which participants are engaging in the assessment of teacher candidates with the new performance-based instruments. Since the mentors agreed to assess the candidates in this way, you would not be asking them to do additional work. Further, you would not be asking them to examine the ways in which they are using performance-based assessment with the children in their classes. In this way, you would be asking the teachers to participate in an inquiry process that for them is less risky, less time-consuming, and more connected to what they believe is their role. (March 9, 2000).

After reading Judith's comments, I realized I could no longer operate in a bubble when I was at the PDS. One of the key challenges for becoming an insider was to learn to take the perspective of a classroom teacher again—

something I had not done in 25 years! I had to examine my expectations and focus more on the *process* of my work rather than on what I had hoped to be the final product. Making decisions jointly and collaboratively was key to becoming an insider.

I replied to Judith's suggestions with the following:

> Regarding your comments about how the mentor teachers might be feeling right now—I think you're right about the part of their possibly feeling threatened. Until now, the focus at [the school] has been on the teacher candidates. As you said, it's part of the PDS agreement. However, what was proposed for our inquiry project goes beyond that. Only a couple of teachers were included in the steering committee's discussion of what our focus should be. What confounds the situation is that I'm new at [the school]. Due to my involvement with the NCATE project, I'm now supervising interns there (along with a colleague from my department who has worked there for the past year and is "easing me" into the new context). I think if I had already established some previous track record of trust and rapport with the mentors, things may have turned out differently.

> Good news, though, is that three more mentors gave their consent today! The principal also told me that he's "talking it up" with them and that some more will come around. As a newcomer to [the PDS], it seems to me that is the culture of the place, and if I'm patient and we all get to know each other better, things will begin to play out differently. (March 9, 2000).

Starting with What I Know I Can Do

My primary focus as a researcher at a PDS site was on conducting inquiry and figuring out how to include all the members of the partnership in the process. As I traveled deeper into the realities of the PDS, I became more aware of some of the diversity issues in the school. Like many urban schools, the PDS had a predominantly African American student population but only a handful of African American teachers. This reality became apparent to me as I tried to recruit more teachers into the inquiry project.

This awareness was shared with Judith:

> Although only six out of the 15 mentor teachers decided to participate in the project, I'm feeling better about it now. I realized when I was at the school yesterday that all of the mentor teachers who are African American (three of them) chose to participate. This makes me feel good personally because I know I have a way of establishing trust with minority women who are teachers. When I taught for four years at an off-campus location in southeastern Virginia, I gained a reputation for successfully helping minority graduate students who were in leadership positions in schools.

> I guess what I'm trying to get at is that if one of the issues concerning PDS is diversity, then I think we need to ensure that ALL members (including teachers of color) have access to quality professional development. By having a dialogue with the three minority (as well as the three majority) teachers, I hope to give them a chance to think more deeply about their teaching and experience as a mentor.
>
> My colleague who has been the university supervisor at [the PDS] for the past year (my "key informant") pointed out that many of the veteran teachers have not experienced the "reflective practitioner" model that new teachers have experienced. My guess is that having to write something about their teaching may be pretty scary for the older teachers. With that in mind, I'm going to take the time to write back to them every week in order to provide additional support. (March 17, 2000).

Judith replied:

> After reading your note a second time this morning what struck me was the part where you indicated that you will be "writing back" to the teachers weekly. I believe that the teachers will welcome your engagement; in fact, given the minimal feedback that most teachers receive, your input may be critical to them. I know that PDS participants sometimes provide this kind of feedback to each other, but that is not always the case in busy schools. Further, most folks continue to be reluctant to exchange ideas with each other in a regular and systematic way. (March 20, 2000).

When I read this response from Judith, my hopes for becoming a PDS insider were bolstered. Without her encouraging comments, I may have dismissed my writing back to the teachers as being nothing special. I did not realize I was building on something valuable from my past practices as a teacher-educator and that these practices could make a contribution to the PDS. At this point, I felt I was at least headed in the right direction for becoming an insider in the school, and specifically, with the teachers.

Becoming Trustworthy in Their Eyes

My position in the PDS as a researcher was endorsed at the political level because of the school's agreement to participate in the NCATE project. It was why I was there. However, my acceptance as an insider at the personal and professional levels still had a long way to go. After several months of planning the inquiry project, partly with others and partly alone, I was still uneasy in my relationships with the teachers. The principal encouraged the teachers to participate in the research project, but he and I had very little interaction with each other at that point. I think the PDS expected me to do the

"Research" (with a capital "R") and that would be the end of it. During the data collection phase of the project, I learned I would become the supervisor of teacher candidates for the following year. The success of this new role would be predicated upon becoming an insider (or not) over the next few months. In order to do a good job of supervising teacher candidates, I first had to make sure that teachers found me to be a trustworthy colleague in their eyes.

I wrote to Judith:

> Things are going better now for me at [the school]. Although there are only five mentor teachers doing the weekly reflections for the inquiry project, I think people are beginning to see me as an ally and a support for them. I think part of what I'm experiencing is that the university supervisors have never really worked with the mentor teachers in a supervisory or consultative way. In other words, mentor teachers may take a graduate course taught by a university supervisor, but they do not necessarily look upon the university person as one who would be a friendly critic or consultant to them.

> There are two modes, I think: university supervisors supervise [teacher candidates] and teach graduate courses. That's it. Three-way conversations with the mentor teachers, teacher candidates, and university faculty only occur when there is a problem with the student teacher—it is not part of the standard procedure. Thus, my "intervention" as friendly critic or consultant has now changed that dynamic, at least for a few. (April 11, 2000).

At this point, I still felt like more of an outsider than an insider, but through my persistence in involving teachers in the process of conducting the research, subtle changes began to occur. A significant event happened when I obtained permission to interview some children for the project. This was a collaborative effort on the part of the site coordinator (assistant principal), the third and fifth grade teachers, and the district's director of assessment and accountability. Within a few days, the teachers had obtained the necessary permissions from parents, and the district office supported the project.

I shared my "triumph" with Judith in the following:

> Last week I conducted two focus groups for the [NCATE] project. One with third graders and one with fifth graders. Both groups had recently taken the [state assessments]. With the help of the PDS coordinator, I devised some questions that basically asked the children to tell me what they had learned about doing certain performances in reading and writing. Frankly, neither she nor I are experts on the topic because we don't teach it, but we put the questions together as best we could. Also, because the director of assessment and accountability for [the county] wanted to see the questions in writing. The questions were approved post haste.

The interesting thing that happened during the actual focus groups was that the mentor teacher [who worked with non-tenured teachers in the building] agreed to be with me while I interviewed the children. As I started interviewing the third graders, it was apparent my questions to them were not clear because they asked me for clarification. I deferred to the mentor teacher, who in turn, did an excellent job of interviewing the children! She skillfully reworded the questions which the PDS coordinator and I had so crudely put together! It was amazing to witness because, suddenly, the research was really becoming COLLABORATIVE!!!

In addition, the PDS coordinator popped in to observe the conversation and added some questions and comments of her own. Because both of them know the children and the kinds of activities that were done this year, they did a good job of using "kid friendly" terminology that elicited fuller responses from the children.

My wish is that the teachers will engage in some form of action research that will help open their eyes to the cultural aspects of performance assessment. I believe that their current technical training in performance assessment may mask some of the underlying issues of diversity. Because there is so much emphasis on how to design and implement an assessment, emphasis on child development, learning and motivation is often overlooked. I know this is especially true for the teacher candidates. Although they are very skilled in writing the assessments as beginning teachers, their implementation of the assessments belies their lack of expertise in motivating the children and sustaining that motivation for a long period of time (which the assessments require). (June 5, 2000).

As the inquiry project for NCATE came to a close, I knew I was on my way to becoming an insider. However, because I had worked as a classroom teacher for only a short time many years ago, I felt somewhat unprepared to deal with the school's administration. The bulk of my teaching career had been in higher education where I had spent 15 years in the liberal arts and teacher education. I had worked professionally with many school administrators as a course instructor, dissertation advisor, or university consultant, but I had not worked *collaboratively* with any administrators in a real-life school setting. For me, being under someone else's roof seemed to change the personal dynamics and rules of the game. Creating a counterculture and trying to negotiate its parameters were not easy for me. I also struggled with my efforts to make joint decision making a part of the norm in the PDS.

Again, I shared some thoughts with Judith:

During the past few days, I have spent a great deal of time at [the PDS]. I think I am now much more of an insider than when I started working with the school last January. This week I presented preliminary findings from the inquiry project to the entire staff. I'm not sure what they thought of it. There were no questions from the group, and the principal told me that the lack of response should not be interpreted as a negative sign. Hopefully, I will have other opportunities to find out what they think about it.

The principal included me in an administrators' meeting. It was the first time in my life that I attended such a meeting. It gave me new insights into the relationship between teachers and administrators at [the school]. The emphasis this year is "writing in the content areas." This will supplement the previous emphasis on performance assessment (the state assessment is primarily a writing test). So, literacy is now in vogue...(September 1, 2000).

Finally, Being Honest

Throughout 2000–2002, I continued to serve as the university liaison at the PDS. I was fully responsible each year for leading a cohort of 16 teacher candidates in a one-year internship in the PDS. This included teaching preservice courses on site, supervising the candidates, consulting with mentor teachers, coordinating activities with the school's administration, and conducting meetings in collaboration with the site coordinator. During this time, I knew I was more of an insider, not so much because the administration consulted with me on important decisions but because my relationship with the teachers had definitely begun to change. *Being honest* in our relationships also became an indicator for being an insider.

In my third year at the school, the excitement of the NCATE Project had passed, and I had settled into my teaching and supervision duties. My relationship with the teachers and administrators had changed as a result of our knowing a little more about each other. That summer, the principal's mother died, and I attended the funeral services with the other teachers and staff. We all became closer as we shared in our principal's loss. On that occasion, I realized I had become a true member of the school's staff because *I saw myself and the others saw me* in a new light. This had nothing to do with joint decision-making or collaboration. It was a moment in time when our *caring* for each other was manifested publicly and was carried beyond the schoolhouse.

When I returned to the PDS in the fall, I *felt* that I had become an insider at a very *personal* level. On a professional level, I was also becoming more of an insider. By working with the site coordinator to schedule a series of meetings held during school hours, the teachers and administrators began to take a more active role in planning collaborative activities. These included the teacher candidates' portfolio review, a community service project, and an action research project.

A turning point for me occurred at the following point:

> The mentor teachers and I discuss the format for the Portfolio Review, how the portfolios will be evaluated. [The principal and assistant principal] give input on the community service project. They would like the [teacher candidates] to help with the Math Facts program. I agree and ask if we could use the data from the project as our action research [required during student teaching]. [The principal]] says OK. He has returned from staff development [where he has heard Michael Fullan, a famous researcher/school reformer speak]. He seems motivated. He says there are many more PDSs now, and we need to work at staying as a leader in the movement.

> He asks, does anyone know what action research is? [A teacher who presented with me at a research conference] asks, isn't that what we did when we presented our papers at the conference? I say yes. Also, I point out that the School Improvement Plan is the outline for an action research project. We just need to focus on one strand of it, collect data, and analyze/share it with the wider community. [The assistant principal] nods in agreement. This is a big breakthrough. Also, it is public. (December 4, 2001).

I was delighted after this meeting because I felt that all the right pieces were finally in place to achieve joint decision making on important aspects of the partnership, including action research. The principal had been very *honest* when he asked whether or not anyone knew what action research was. Until then, action research had been conducted only by the teacher candidates as part of their student teaching and had not been a joint endeavor of the school and the university. As I had suspected, there was misunderstanding about action research, and without the principal's endorsement, it would never become a vehicle for collaboration and joint decision making at the *political* level. By raising an honest question in front of the whole group, the principal had opened the possibilities for change at a higher level. I left the meeting that day feeling that at last I was becoming an insider on all fronts in the PDS.

Greg: "Transforming the Veteran into a PDS Advocate"

Ever since I can remember, I have been the outsider. In junior high, high school and college, I was the rebel (mostly with a cause, or so I thought), the one who valued honesty and commitment above all else. Of my peers, I was one of the first and one of the few in a very small Southern conservative rural high school to oppose the Vietnam War. In college, I edited the campus underground newspaper, demonstrated against a variety of causes, and volunteered in poverty programs. One of my earliest positions was as a teacher in a low-income minority school, and then I earned my stripes in Head Start programs. In all of the circumstances, I never aspired to be the "insider."

Since 1989, I have been working at the university. I am a veteran. I have started student teaching centers (our pre-PDS sites), picked up the pieces of a PDS experiencing broken communication and animosity within the partnership, and begun a new professional development school partnership between the city and county school systems. For the past 13 years, my role has been to supervise seniors during their pre-student teaching and student teaching experiences. The transformation of a college student or intern into a teacher candidate captivates me. The transformation of young adults or what I call "becoming a teacher" is what makes my work interesting, fun, challenging, and, most of all, worthwhile. While still a student of the transformation process after all these years as a university supervisor (and seven years as an elementary school principal watching it happen to teachers), my role as a university supervisor was always clearly defined.

The role concentrated on the development of teachers and working in partnership with mentor teachers and principals of elementary schools to establish a process and create an environment to nurture the transformation from intern to teacher. Motivating and challenging interns to reach within themselves, to aspire to become teachers, transcend all other responsibilities.

In the words of one former intern,

> Our supervisor scared us. On our first day, those of us who wanted to be teachers realized he really wanted us not just to be teachers, but to be great teachers, the teachers we had dreamed of being. After he scared the s*** out of us, we spent the semester demonstrating how much we already knew and what we were actually capable of. None of us knew that we knew how to be teachers but during our last semester, we became teachers or we did not finish the semester.

In keeping with my outsider image, I never worried about anything except the welfare of the interns and their development as teachers. The time and energy necessary to supervise the interns, work with mentor teachers, fulfill university commitments, write about the transforming process, and be a husband and father consumed me. In the beginning, as a university supervisor in the old student teaching center (pre-PDS), I considered myself a guest in someone's house when I entered a school building. It never occurred to me I wanted to be an insider; my role as an insider was on the university campus. Even now, though my role had to change because of the PDS, I still value my time as the outsider. It was and still is hard to see all of the advantages of being an insider.

I began my journey as a PDS coordinator in 1997, almost by accident. In 1996, the university and the school system had established a joint appointment for a school system employee. This person had little or no university teaching experience, but she had a great reputation within the school system. She handled her first year of the joint appointment with a great deal of success, yet she had never taught seniors. The members of our department were concerned about her ability to supervise the transformation process, to teach the courses, and serve as a liaison for the PDS site. Thus, I became her collaborator.

During that summer, we realized our new PDS site had experienced a series of missed communications with the previous university supervisors. We fixed the so-called problem easily. Our jointly appointed person became the insider while I was free to concentrate on the development of interns. Although I learned a great deal about the PDS site from this colleague, I remained safely within the confines of the university. She soon realized the previous university supervisors had developed a great PDS site, and with our team effort, we had an award-winning PDS. It was her devotion to PDS that resulted in an application for the Association of Teacher Educators (ATE) award as the national Outstanding Teacher Education Program, an award we received.

Together, we set the goal of demonstrating the collaboration between us and valuing collaboration between the school and the university. By our collaboration, we demonstrated a partnership of great success with high standards, effective communications, and significantly higher expectations. We graduated a fine group of 15 interns; 13 became teachers.

We started planning for the coming school year. The plan was for her to work again to develop a group of juniors whom we would jointly supervise during their senior year. We understood how our collaboration could help to improve both of us in many ways. As I went on sabbatical, we looked forward to several years of working together.

Typically in a PDS partnership, change is inevitable and often sudden. By the Summer, she had transferred to a new position in the school system, and a newly hired assistant professor with no PDS experience took her place. And I was preparing to go on sabbatical. The PDS year ended with further disaster, including the new faculty member leaving the university with the new group of interns facing the uncertainty of another trauma.

The goals that had been accomplished in the previous couple of years now lay in ruins. Fortunately, I had a good reputation with the school, and we elected to begin again. A second year of starting from scratch meant no progress in going beyond the beginning. Nevertheless, I had to think about what it would take to become the dreaded "insider." But, I was able to work closely with the PDS school site liaison leaving me free to concentrate on the interns. As this year ended, I realized that I had learned several things about becoming an "insider " and that many of the decisions I had made were "insider" decisions.

My reflection at the end of the year included journal entries such as,

> …by working with [the principal], we made several decisions that enhanced the academic achievement of the children and the interns. Our focus and our problem solving actually cemented the partnership at the PDS. While the partnership lacked the depth that it needed, we had established a relationship that made the partnership sustainable and reasonable to continue. With the level of commitment demonstrated by both sides, we could withstand the upcoming NCATE evaluation and field test. While there would be weaknesses in our PDS, the initial partnership was strong and viable.

And,

> While my role as a university faculty member has changed forever because of my PDS work, I do not ever want to return to the old ways. The days of not being involved in the fabric of the school community, of not being dedicated to school reform are over. However, if I am to become part of a PDS, then I have to begin my own PDS. I have to find a way to actually become involved in the important decisions, not just be on the outside looking in.

My fourth year working in PDS found me mentoring a new faculty member at my former PDS and developing a new site. My new colleague took over my previous PDS site while I spent the year starting a new PDS. I was lucky enough to find two principals who immediately trusted me and I trusted them. From the beginning, the principals at both schools involved me in critical decisions such as hiring the PDS site coordinators, selecting mentor teachers, determining class sizes, shifting personnel in each school, analyzing test score results, planning and conducting research, and working in staff development. One area was off limits by my request, my observations of the teachers in the school: what I see and hear from the teachers stays confidential, and both principals have respected my feelings on this issue. At both schools, I have a faculty mailbox and I am listed on the faculty rosters. Many teachers ask my advice, and we often discuss issues related to teaching. The voices of the teachers and the children in the school become my concern along with my concern for the interns. Reforming and changing the school as well as improving the teaching and learning environment has become our mission.

My involvement in decision making as it relates to teaching and the transformation process of the interns helps me to see how I fit into the school setting. The amount of time and preparation necessary to achieve this insider status is significant. Further, this work has forever changed my role at the university and the role of my fellow faculty members. While our discussions still focus on interns and classes, we have little if any time to engage in traditional forms of scholarship or traditional faculty responsibilities. We spend our time in the school buildings grappling with issues related to schools and rarely have the chance to debate issues. In many ways, we have become isolated from campus colleagues and from the life on the campus. Moreover, in many ways this is the case for our students. We are no longer part of the campus; we are a part of the school. In some ways, we are in a twilight zone with campus responsibilities including committee work, advising, and traditional scholarship yet with great allegiances to schools. Some of us have adapted better than others. However, our departmental colleagues have recognized our work and time commitment, and they support our efforts.

Becoming a PDS insider is still not in my life plans. I do not relish the meetings, the gossip, the inside jokes, and some other aspects of being an insider. My insider status is still based on relationships with the school staff members and how the interns feel about the school. In her first weekly reflection, one of the interns wrote,

> For the first time, I am in a school-based field experience where I am welcomed, where my professor knows the teachers and they know him. Everything has been set up in advance for me to be successful. If I am not successful, it will be for reasons other than those that have prevented me from having fulfilling past field experiences.

Again, the most important advantage is for the interns. As they return after the semester break, their reflections are filled with enthusiasm for returning, seeing the children's bright faces, and facing the challenges of their final semester. Another intern wrote:

It has been exciting and rewarding to be able to return to the first grade at [the] elementary school. The students' enthusiasm for my return was more than welcoming. I was particularly surprised to hear "difficult" students tell me how much they missed me while I was gone. The students' excitement paired with my rejuvenated spirit and the welcoming attitude of my mentor teacher gave me a new and improved outlook on teaching. It was apparent, once again, how rewarding teaching can be.

And,

It is hard to believe that we only have eight more days here at [the] school. I have learned a great deal during my time here, and I am going to miss the relationships that I have built with my colleagues and students. We are planning a China Day for my last day to go hand in hand with my Reading/Social Studies lessons on other countries. It should be great; we are ordering Chinese food in and are going to have them sitting on the floor for the experience. I think it will be a time to remember for the children and for me.

During the senior year, the interns have become the "insiders." They are now closer to their mentor teachers and the teaching staff than they are to me. In fact, the interns have become the insiders, and, luckily for me, I remain more of the outsider, a role that makes me more comfortable. While my role is unlike that of other faculty members outside the College of Education, I still feel that I have held true to my goal of successfully transforming the interns. They have become teachers, accepting the challenges of changing the lives of others in the most meaningful of ways.

Last summer, my colleagues made me the chairperson of our department. As a result, I do not have to face the problem of how to become more of an "insider." My own development in this regard will end. The transformation from an outsider to insider will not be complete as I assume a new role in our department and leave, temporarily, the PDS site. In a few years, when I return to a PDS site, I will be the veteran, a little older, still the "outsider" and maybe a little wiser, but still "starting over."

Nechie: "The University PDS Liaison as a Resistant Immigrant"

Before 1998, I was a full-time, tenured, university faculty member whose primary teaching assignment involved supervising undergraduate student teachers placed in two elementary schools and teaching their final curriculum seminar. As a teacher-center supervisor, I was an outsider in the public schools. I was more than a traveler or a tourist, however, since I spent so much time in the setting and had become a familiar presence to teachers and children. Typically, they accepted my presence in the classroom without question, although I did once overhear a fourth grader ask his friend, "Who *is* she?" "I don't know," replied his friend. "She comes and watches." The first child was incredulous and responded, "She gets paid for just watching!?" So, though my purpose might have been opaque to some classroom participants, my presence was not unusual.

If I was not a traveler or a tourist, perhaps I was a trader. I brought student teachers expertise in classroom management, curriculum development, and instructional delivery and a small stipend for cooperating teachers. I traded these commodities for the opportunity to include my students in classrooms and the assistance of the cooperating teachers in the students' training. In addition, I built professional relationships and personal friendships with teachers and grew as a professional myself.

After several years, I was given a mailbox and a small space in each school to keep my lunch and my books when I was in the building. At this time, I became more than a trader. I became a resident alien. I spent most of my working hours in the teacher center, and I had a place in the life of each school. Even so, I knew that my work life was anchored within my department on the college campus. I did not change my primary affiliation or my primary identity, and nobody suggested that I should. In the public schools, I was a comfortable outsider satisfied working within classrooms with students and cooperating teachers. On the university campus, I was an insider who understood the culture and worked happily within it.

I knew that *The Redesign of Teacher Education in Maryland* (1995) required all colleges and universities to create professional development schools, and, at the request of my department chairperson, I had developed a plan to implement this transition in the district where I had teacher centers. My plan called for opening the first PDS in 2006, but the enthusiasm of the district's superintendent for the PDS model put my plan on the fast track. When the associate dean called me into his office and said, "Here's a deal you can't refuse," he was right. The weight and resources of the school system were behind the immediate implementation of my plan, and, before I knew it, I was the university coordinator of a fledgling PDS.

This would be my first experience in a PDS, my university's first PDS in the district, and the district's first experience with an undergraduate PDS.

It was also the first time either institution had established a PDS for students planning to graduate in January. I was promised a great adventure.

It was my understanding that the main difference between a teacher center and a PDS was the emphasis on in-service teacher education, funds to implement programs, opportunities for research, and a governance structure that placed leadership opportunities in the hands of teachers. In addition, I realized that even more of my work life would now take place in the schools. I anticipated that my teaching tasks would remain the same but that a significant number of administrative tasks would be added to my workload.

Our first year was an extremely busy one. Two other university faculty members and I taught four methods courses in the school buildings, and I supervised the interns' year-long internship in mentors' classrooms. We instituted an active program of providing in-service opportunities to groups of teachers and to individuals. The half-time facilitator the school system assigned to the PDS and I met with teachers to help them understand the ways the PDS could assist them in reaching the professional goals stated in their yearly goal statements. The PDS also sponsored mentor training, a series of on-site workshops with the Maryland Writing Project, and an intensive reading initiative as part of a nationwide effort sponsored by the National Council of Teachers of English.

During the first year of the PDS, teachers and principals chaired the governance meetings on a rotating schedule. Building-based committees met monthly and included the principal, three teachers, the PDS facilitator, and me. A joint steering committee made up of representatives from each school met monthly. The district's director of professional development schools attended these meetings and provided considerable leadership for our efforts at accomplishing goals, finding funds, and clarifying issues.

Our first cohort of student interns graduated that January amidst much hoopla, and I felt proud of our accomplishments. It seemed to me that the elements I had anticipated as being part of a PDS were, in fact, in place. I continued to find great satisfaction in teaching and supervising interns and in working with mentor teachers. Our graduates had become justifiably confident young teachers, and several had begun their careers in their own first classrooms immediately upon graduation.

The administrative tasks I had anticipated were evident and with my teaching assignments created a workload that was, at times, overwhelming. By the time our PDS welcomed its second group of interns, I began to feel exhausted by administrative concerns. The most serious issue was finding instructional space in the school buildings for the classes the university offered the interns. There was no lack of commitment on the part of the principals to house the university courses, but the space issue could not be solved because school buildings were overcrowded, and the school system refused to leave the trailer we had used our first year on the school grounds. Since we were a PDS, the university did not provide space on campus. During the second year, we taught at a high school a mile from the PDS. The issue of finding suitable space remained problematic semester after semester.

In addition to the concern about administrative tasks and the issue about space, several other issues were becoming apparent to me. First, I realized that some PDS participants did not consider my "home culture" relevant to our working together. The school system's timetable could not accommodate the university's need to plan a semester in advance. Some university traditions were seen as "ivory tower," and my claim to special expertise was dismissed. The university was valued for the resources and opportunities it could provide, but in all other things, the school system's perspective was considered more germane.

Every semester in the PDS, the district's director of professional development schools or the school system's PDS facilitator assigned to our PDS told me I should be sharing the responsibility for the instruction and supervision of interns. Each semester, I had to defend my expertise and responsibility in this area. Although I consulted with the mentor teachers and used their suggestions in revising my courses, and often I asked teachers to present particular topics in the curriculum seminar, I refused to let a PDS committee write the syllabi for my courses. Similarly, I always made the interns' classroom placements in consultation with the principals. However, I resisted the district's staff development office's frequent suggestion that a PDS committee should set the policies for intern placements. As a university faculty member with many years of successful experience, I believed my training and expertise in university teaching and supervision as well as my responsibility to assign grades and clear interns for graduation made it obvious I should be responsible for the interns' instruction and supervision.

Second, I realized that I defined and approached my PDS tasks differently from the way others involved in the PDS defined and approached their tasks. I believed my job as a PDS coordinator was to facilitate the accomplishments of others. Since I worked for the university, I believed I did not need to make myself visible in the school system. Early in 1999, I wrote in my journal:

> I see my role as one of working behind the scenes, and making things happen, and getting lots of other people involved. That's not the culture of the school. In this setting, everybody wants to be visible and to take credit for things...there is nothing selfless about their work in the PDS. Everybody is building a fiefdom and making their reputations. I had no idea it would be like this.

In addition, as an outsider, habitual patterns of behavior did not have the influence on me that they had for everybody else in the school setting. I often questioned things that nobody else around me found unusual. For example, I first met the district's director of PDS initiatives at a meeting of a PDS advisory group. This group had been meeting at the central office to draft policy documents for the several professional development schools the district planned to initiate in the coming school year. My journal entry recorded the event:

> This is the first time she attended a meeting of this group. By the time she finished this meeting we were no longer an advisory board; we were now a group that met to exchange ideas, and we no longer met at the board of education; now we met at various schools or at the staff development center. After the meeting she stopped me and said that she wanted to be at all the meetings I had with the principals at my schools. When I asked why, she was surprised.

I soon realized that she was not accustomed to being asked to share reasons for her decisions, and my resistance to her request that I tell her in advance of all the meetings I planned to hold with administrators was novel in her experience. It signaled an independence on my part that was not part of the ethos of the school system. At the time I did not understand her need to control the sprawling PDS network she was charged with administering. She had to defend her budget and prove the importance of her work to several layers of administrators above her. From her point of view, she could do this best by monitoring the activities of those below her, and she included me in that group.

I had assumed I would be independent in assisting the PDS in arriving at our definition of what our partnership meant to us. And since I believed that teachers are our reason for existence, I believed that primary decision making should be in their hands. Yet at the beginning of our second year, the PDS director decided that our PDS "overdid governance last year." Our schedule of meetings was cut in half. Further, the half-time facilitator now chaired all the meetings. By the end of our fourth year, only one teacher from each school attended the governance meetings, and rarely did they make comments. To my disappointment, the governance structure no longer emphasized the leadership or the participation of teachers.

If I felt out of step with school system administrators, I was also losing touch with my university colleagues. Now that I spent four days a week in the field at the PDS, I had little time on campus. My loss of contact with my university colleagues robbed me of my professional support system and an important source of my intellectual life. The better the job I did at the PDS, the less I was on campus. Yet the nature and extent of this extra work were poorly understood. Campus administrators told me that the success of my PDS "goes without saying," while they criticized me for neglecting to volunteer for additional tasks on campus and for failing to maintain a presence at conferences and in academic publications. My lack of visibility in the school system was by design, but my lack of visibility on campus was the result of circumstances. In a journal entry at this time, I noted:

> In the school system my accomplishments are unrecognized or co-opted and on campus, they are invisible. I am…sick and tired of always having to defend myself.

At this time, the benefits of the PDS for faculty members eluded me. I wondered if I were a poor match for PDS work. Still, I enjoyed supervising interns and working with mentor teachers, and my success and satisfaction as a teacher center coordinator had seemed to augur well for my comfort as a PDS coordinator. I now realize that part of my discomfort had a less obvious source, and it had to do with the expectation that I would change the sort of outsider I was and my resistance to that expectation.

At the outset, I had been an established resident alien in the school culture, accepted by school personnel as somebody who came and went and yet belonged. This perception did not change among the teachers in the school, and my good relationships with them persisted and grew closer. But the central office personnel with whom I had had no prior relationship and, to a lesser extent, other administrators believed I had changed my status. They believed that I had become an immigrant.

As an immigrant, I was invited to join the host culture. But I refused to become a genuine immigrant and submerge myself in the school culture. I chose not to make our close working relationship a reason to identify with the goals and demands of the school system. Rather, I liked being a university professor and chose not to adopt the professional perspectives and cultural orientations of the public school administrators with whom I worked. This created a sense of distance and caution in my dealings with them that stood in stark contrast to the ease and friendliness of my relationships with the teachers in the buildings.

For the central office administrators in our setting, the behavior of an outsider who refuses to become assimilated though she spends 80% of her work life in the setting probably seemed inexplicable. Since I was unwilling to become a genuine immigrant and substitute the perspective of the school system for my perspective as a university faculty member, I remained, for them, an obvious (and stubborn) outsider.

This meant that I did not know what "transformation" might be in this circumstance. The school system is too big; personnel are too well socialized; too many careers are at stake, and the imbalance of the number of school people involved in meetings versus the one university faculty member present made it impossible to shape the school system's point of view about or approach to educational issues. It proved equally impossible to have an impact on the university's definition of a reasonable workload or appropriate teaching space.

The school system was pleased to have the university's help in accomplishing goals as set by the schools in ways approved by the schools. The university was pleased to have the opportunity to train its students in the district. I believed neither institution intended to be transformed by the other.

As the person in the middle, my challenge was to maintain our working relationship while preserving my professional identity. For me, this involved maintaining the independence of an outsider in the public school culture and resisting the school system's desire to absorb me. After four years, the energy this demanded in conjunction with the growing sense that I was becoming an outsider in the college community led me to request a change in my teaching responsibilities.

Lauren: "PDS as a Catalyst for Change"

I grew up in the community in which I teach, giving me the privilege of teaching children of high school classmates. I have always cared deeply for children. And, I used to say, "You could put me in a room with one hundred children and I'd be happy to teach and entertain them, but in a room with five adults, I'd be petrified." You will later see how this has changed.

I began my career teaching pre-kindergarten. The school had just become a professional development school, not that I knew what that meant. The partnership did not include internships for early childhood majors, and I did not become fully immersed in the PDS climate until my third year of teaching when I began teaching first grade. My first mentoring experience was an incredible one. My first intern and I had a wonderful rapport, and it was refreshing to see someone so eager to learn. She was hired at the school and now serves as a mentor herself.

During my nine years as a part of the PDS, I have had many opportunities to become immersed in the PDS climate: taking graduate courses, attending conferences, mentoring interns, and teaching a class for the University. These experiences and opportunities have caused many changes in my personal and professional life. A description of these changes follow.

Role Shifting

The role shifts that occur in a professional development school are much like the magician's handkerchief trick. The magician begins with one large handkerchief. The handkerchief is hidden and then slowly revealed as a long chain of brightly colored handkerchiefs.

I began my career as an early childhood educator. This is a vitally important role in stimulating young minds, but I did not have much involvement with PDS. Later, I added the new role of "learner" when I began taking graduate courses on-site with colleagues. This was an opportunity to network with other PDS teachers and to learn some "fresh ideas" to add to my teaching repertoire. Next, I became a mentor teacher for junior and senior interns. This added the role of mentor to that of reflective practitioner. This caused me to look closely at my teaching in order to be the best model and trainer.

The next role I began to fill for the PDS was one I never saw myself in as an adjunct faculty member for the university. In Fall semester 2000, I became the second classroom teacher to teach ELED 429, Reading Assessment to the interns in a PDS. Now, I am a teacher and a teacher of teachers.

The last role that I have undertaken thus far is in leadership. For example, I have had the opportunity to present at many professional conferences, most recently (2002) the Annual Summer Conference of the Association of Teacher Educators that was held in Williamsburg, Virginia. Also, I have conducted many PDS site visits for the PDS partnership. The young woman who was afraid to present to five adults is now an experienced professional who is comfortable sharing information with large groups. Each role I have undertaken in our PDS is like one of the magician's brightly colored handkerchiefs. Each is important in holding the chain together; each is vibrant and unique.

A Change in Attitudes Toward Universities and PDS

When you attend a magic show, you do so without knowledge of the inner workings of each trick. This can lead to confusion and curiosity. When (if) the magician decides to reveal the secrets of his trade, you have that "aha" moment.

Working in a PDS has given me many "aha" moments, mostly in my attitudes toward universities and PDS as a whole. First, I have a new respect for professors. As a college student, I was not aware of the work involved in planning two and a half hours of meaningful learning during a course session. When I took on the responsibility of teaching ELED 429, I was given an outline of what was to be taught and a textbook. From that, I have had to create a semester-long program of study. I spent many hours trying to plan engaging lessons for the interns to be able to keep them challenged and interested in the subject matter. Also, I needed to be a "subject master." Well-educated adults know much more than first-graders! Fortunately, I have had the opportunity to work closely with university faculty members who combine their syllabi, play to one another's strengths, network, and join together to prepare the best new teachers we can.

Through this work, I have come to realize the additional demands on the time of university faculty as they conduct research, publish, and pursue their quest for tenure. In addition, I see that they do want to know what new teachers will have as challenges. The university faculty members involved with our PDS spend time visiting classrooms and getting to know teachers. This releases them from the bubble of teaching theory to help them integrate theory with current practices.

In this time, my perceptions of PDS have changed. Before my involvement with the interns, I could only draw from my own student teaching experiences. I was happy to have been placed in two completely different schools for student teaching. Originally, I thought that PDS negated the importance of getting to know how and why different schools operate in different ways. Also, I did my student teaching in the Spring semester and had no concept of how to set-up a classroom at the start of the school year. I always wondered, How do I teach these four-year-olds to walk in a line?

Now, I have seen the light, aha! Through the PDS, I have seen how interns are immersed into the culture of the school. They are learning how a classroom works and the role of each individual classroom in the total school. They meet families, help mentors setup the classroom, observe the first day of school, attend committee meetings, and learn the real-life demands on teachers.

Changes in Self

The magician turns a rubber bird into a healthy live bird, which promptly flies away. I am that bird.

The greatest changes the PDS brought to my life have been on a personal level. I have been transformed from a shy, unsure beginning teacher to a confident, experienced teacher/mentor/reflective practitioner/college instructor/leader. The professional development opportunities I have engaged in through the PDS have challenged me and encouraged me to "think outside the box." I have learned and experimented with new theories and strategies from Fred Jones, Steven Covey, Jay McTighe, Howard Gardner, and others. Presenting at conferences on behalf of the PDS partnership has given me valuable experience in collaboration and in public speaking. PDS site visits have also been of value, helping me learn about other schools in our state, our nation, and even in other countries. Teaching ELED 429 has helped me take flight. I enjoy teaching adults and could possibly pursue more opportunities in the future. And, I am flying high above the ground now looking for many new opportunities and hidden possibilities.

Maggie: "Concluding Narrative"

In 1995, the Maryland state policy known as the *Redesign of Teacher Education* set in motion a process that has changed teacher preparation programs dramatically. This was the intent. This new transformative model engages P–16 faculty more deeply in the continuous professional development of pre- and in-service teachers. University faculty are transformed as well although these faculty bring forward the very real issue that the time needed for reflection so essential to the transformation process can vanish with added demands a PDS coordinator faces.

I first became involved in PDS work as part of a P–16 team writing a grant that would fund Towson University's initial PDS. My office was located next to that of one of Towson's first PDS coordinators, so I was able to witness firsthand what was involved in being a PDS coordinator. Now at the Maryland State Department of Education, I have expanded my PDS involvement, working with P–16 faculty, many of who—are my former colleagues at the university and its P–12 partner schools.

Since 1995, the state has sought and received funds to support PDS at the institutional and state level. In addition, Maryland has a PDS Network that sponsors conferences, conducts leadership academies, and, most importantly, has involved P–16 PDS practitioners in the development of the Maryland PDS Standards, which are now an integral part of the state program approval and accreditation process. As the PDS movement in Maryland grew, there was a call for guidance. Maryland's PDS Standards provide a framework for universities and local school systems to use allowing partnerships to develop that are unique to their relationship, both within and among higher education institutions.

As with all policies, it is those who are working directly with teacher candidates and in-service teachers, the university faculty and P–12 mentor teachers who make the magic happen. For those who were there at the beginning of the PDS movement, there were no role models and there was no handbook. Their actions were guided by their motivation to attempt a new way of providing an extensive and intensive teacher preparation experience, and part of the magic involved the transformation of in-service teachers such as Lauren into leaders within their schools and respected adjunct faculty in the university community. There is something magical about transformation for interns but also for their university supervisors and mentor teachers.

The three university faculty and P–12 adjunct faculty member who have shared their experiences in this chapter bring forward issues my PDS colleagues and I have witnessed statewide. Being in a PDS provides great opportunity for P–12 teachers to grow personally and professionally. Lauren, for example, chose to take on a new challenge, seeking to transform her own professional identity. She serves as a role model for other P–12 teachers, demonstrating their contributions to teacher preparation are recognized and valued. However, Jane, Greg, and Nechie were not hired with the expectation

132   Traditions, Standards, and Transformations

that they would be working as PDS coordinators and, except for Greg, their professional careers have been focused at the university level. Their jobs changed after they were hired. Interestingly, these university faculty members are no longer serving as PDS coordinators although each continues to support the PDS in different ways. Sometimes it is through stepping out of roles that one can be of the most help to those who follow in those roles. As chair, Greg has the opportunity to address issues of training and providing support for PDS coordinators. As Director of Towson University's Institute for Professional Development School Studies, Jane is able to promote PDS research. As a faculty member who was willing to do PDS work but has now returned to campus full-time, Nechie can encourage faculty who remain on campus to provide support for their colleagues who are not always physically present.

A magic trick that seems effortless is the result of planning, trials and attempts that sometimes do not work, and tenacity. The wand is waved as the signal that the magic trick is ready to be to unveiled to an audience that is challenged to figure out how the magic worked. Sometimes, it seems that the work of PDS faculty is magical. How do they do so much with so little accorded to them in time and resources? Indeed, the role of PDS coordinator is different with added responsibilities and expectations. These four PDS faculty bring forward elements of their experience that are of continuing concern for all who do PDS work, wanting or needing to become an insider in order to become part of the decision-making process. These elements include determining a professional identity, tapping into the wisdom of past experiences, building relationships, establishing trust, and fostering communication. Throughout all of this, a PDS coordinator must be honest personally and with others. If things are not working well, that needs to be acknowledged.

For those who are committed to the development of teachers, one cannot underestimate the importance of professional identity. It is this identity that makes one feel comfortable and serves as a barometer of success or leads to feelings and perceptions of failure. It is more difficult to change one's professional identity than to add to it. Lauren's role as adjunct faculty does not change her primary role as a P–12 teacher. She stays in the same place and continues to work with her children. For the university faculty, it is a different story. They leave the university campus where they have been most comfortable and begin a new life as school-based university faculty.

For some, this is an exciting and welcome change, particularly for those who have significant previous P–12 experience. For others, it means giving up strongly held convictions. For all, this precipitates deep personal and professional change.

Past experiences often provide an entry into schools that transcends any formal actions of a PDS coordinator. There is more than one way to become an insider. As someone who works for a state department of education, I could be considered the ultimate outsider; thus I can relate to the experiences that these university faculty have when they begin their work in PDS schools. Building a trusting relationship is a long, difficult, yet ultimately rewarding process. Jane recognized the importance of her experiences with teachers in establishing trust. She demonstrated this most forcefully when she trusted the school faculty to reword her research questions with the children. The teachers knew she saw herself as a researcher who had shared that important piece of her professional identity with them.

Although Greg saw himself as the outsider, as a former principal he seemed to be the most immediately accepted by principals and teachers. They trusted him because they knew he had a true understanding of their real-life experiences, and they could see that he had transferred that same commitment to his teacher candidates. And, he was willing to take on the additional challenge of beginning a new PDS that would involve two local school systems. Nechie had always maintained a significant presence in her teacher centers with the full recognition of all involved that she was a university faculty member, first and foremost. She did not want her professional identity to change, but she was willing to engage the P–12 faculty in the type of collaboration she was accustomed to at the university. Yet, she missed the professional support of colleagues when spending so much time at the school.

The ways in which these faculty members view themselves is reflected in the ways in which they went about building relationships and communication systems. The cultures of the P–12 school and the university set the stage for inevitable conflict and, one hopes, resolution. Each of the university faculty members went into the PDS wanting input in the decision-making process similar to the university ideals of shared governance. Shared governance is not the norm in P–12 schools, where there are definite lines of authority and responsibility. There are levels of acceptance to be sought after—political, professional, and personal. It is difficult, but not impossible, to be an insider with central office staff, building administrators, and classroom teachers, but it is time-consuming. University faculty cannot assume they have immediate acceptance simply by being present in the school building. As these three faculty members demonstrate, it is being present to people in the school that leads to acceptance.

Communication issues are among the most critical in keeping a PDS strong and vibrant. Yet, miscommunication opportunities abound as staff at the P–12 and university level are continually in flux. Every year is a starting over again in some way for PDS relationships. The magic is expected to happen again and again but with different players. University faculty members who are willing to take on this extraordinary challenge and P–12 faculty who want to expand their horizons make the PDS work regardless of the myriad difficulties that arise when dedicated people are working toward something in which they strongly believe. The university is fortunate to have a P–16 PDS community in which faculty members have been willing to leave their comfort zone on behalf of pre-and in-service teachers. For every challenge, there is a success story, a feat of magic that defies full explanation, reflective of the tenacious efforts of the P–16 faculty who endeavor to make this intense collaborative effort work. It is a marvel to perceive.

References

Apple, M. (2001). Market, standards, teaching and teacher education. *Journal of Teacher Education, 52*, 182–196.

Holmes Group (1995). *Tomorrow's schools of education: A report of the Holmes Group.* East Lansing, MI: Author.

Maryland State Department of Education and Maryland Higher Education Commission (1995). *The redesign of teacher education in Maryland.* Annapolis, MD: Authors.

Neapolitan, J., & Harper, S. (2001). *Tying together teacher education and student learning: Results of the NCATE PDS Standards Field Test Project.* Paper presented at the Maryland Professional Development School Network Research Conference, Annapolis, MD.

Teitel, L. (2001). An assessment framework for professional development schools: Going beyond the leap of faith. *Journal of Teacher Education, 52*, 57–69.

Trachtman, R. (1997). The stories of insiders. In M. Levine & R. Trachtman (Eds.), *Making professional development schools work: Politics, practice and policy* (pp. 185–193). New York: Teachers College Press

CHAPTER NINE

Technology Integration Within a Teacher Education Program and a Professional Development School Network

William A. Sadera, David R. Wizer, & Lisa A. Newcomb

For nearly four years, 1999–2003, Towson University's College of Education has been involved in an organized systematic program of faculty development in the area of technology. For three of those years, the college has received federal funding under the Preparing Tomorrow's Teachers to Use Technology (PT³) Program. The purpose of this federally sponsored program is to enhance the skills of faculty so they can integrate technology into teaching with pre-service teacher education students. In this chapter the results of these faculty development efforts with technology in Towson's extensive PDS Network will be featured.

Background

The College of Education was awarded a one-year capacity-building grant in 1999 under the PT³ Program, entitled Standards-Based Technology Integration and Mentoring. The purpose was to develop and implement a faculty-to-faculty mentoring model in order to increase faculty technology integration skills in college methods courses as well as to assist faculty in PDS schools to do the same in their work with pre-service teachers. Based on the success of the mentoring model, the college was awarded a three-year PT³ Implementation grant, Mentoring to Master Technology Integration Project, in 2000, thus expanding the mentor model beyond the College of Education to faculty teaching core teacher preparation courses in the university's College of Liberal Arts and the College of Science and Mathematics.

To participate, faculty must propose a personal project or plan of professional development for the integration of technology in their instruction. To date, 77 faculty members have been supported through this program. Individual faculty members work with teacher education candidates from the College of Education, other colleges at the university (including Liberal Arts and Science and Mathematics), and in Towson's PDS Network (located in 83 public schools in nine Maryland school districts). During the four years, 33 projects have been supported in the College of Education, 12 projects in other colleges at Towson, and 32 projects in the PDS network.

As PDS is at the core of the college's professional preparation of teachers, PDS sites, then, are effective, well-developed partnerships and supportive places for teacher candidates to learn from experienced educators in the schools, not on the university campus. Through this project, opportunities are provided for faculty and teacher candidates to explore and integrate technology effectively in school classrooms, thereby strengthening the curricula. The excellence of the PDS network has been recognized with numerous awards including the Association of Teacher Educators' 1998 recognition as the national "Distinguished Program in Teacher Education."

Mentor Model

A mentor-intern model is used for assisting faculty members as they enhance their use of technology within their teaching. The mentor's role is to support the intern in the integration of technology into the intern's instructional practices and act as an expert in the areas of software use and design, multiple uses of technology, and strategies to integrate technology in teaching.

The intern's role is to design a technology integration project to assist students in a classroom to develop stronger understandings of key curricular and subject area concepts. The intern works with the mentor to design the project, learn how to use the chosen technology, and implement strategies to integrate technology to improve instructional practices. The project design and mentoring takes place at PDS sites in the schools and on campus.

There is support in the literature about mentors assisting teachers in the effective integration of technology in instruction. In an early study on technology integration in schools, MacArthur, Pilato, Kercher, Peterson, Malouf, & Jamison (1995) report on the use of technology mentors to help employ technology in classrooms. In this study skilled mentors [who were teachers] helped novice users employ technology in the classroom.

More recently Kariuki, Franklin, & Duran (2001) among others discussed the benefits for technology partners to enhance their teaching via technology integration. Functioning as experts, mentors provided authentic, experiential learning opportunities and an interpersonal relationship through which social learning can occur (Kariuki, Franklin, & Duran, 2001; Kerka, 1998).

Further, Towson colleagues Wheeler, Wilson, & Berkeley (2001), who were supported in the first year of this project, wrote about the community of learner benefits for their students in teacher education courses at the undergraduate and graduate levels. They discussed the sense of community (established via online discussions with students) and how technology-based discussions allowed students to communicate common experiences and ideas that led to deeper understandings.

Rewards, Support, and Other Benefits

Rewards and benefits have accrued for the College of Education as a result of the project's implementation. First, mentors and interns receive stipends for the work they do on the project, almost all of which is done on time in addition to one's regular responsibilities. One semester, laptop computers were provided to the interns for their use for an academic year. The incentives have served to motivate those on-campus as well as off-campus to spend more time working on their projects. Second, there has been a reciprocal increase in the use of other technology-support resources as a result of participation in the project (as well as afterwards when an intern integrates technology into instruction). In addition, participants have been recognized for their participation in the college and across the university, thus adding to the college's positive reputation for innovations in the use of technology.

As mentioned, there are other supports available to interns, including being able to consult with the other project staff and with faculty liaisons. Further, a range of resources have been made available through the Internet as well as support from an Electronic Learning Community established with our project partner, Johns Hopkins University. This past year, all of the professional development and reporting instruments of the project have been moved to the Internet [see www.towson.edu/tip] for easy access to interns, mentors, and others outside of the project.

An additional benefit to interns is that the work being done with mentors is aligned with the Maryland Teacher Technology Standards. Thus, the materials developed as a result of participation meet these standards, and when implemented at school sites, the schools, too, are effective at achieving these goals. There have been some clear patterns of other benefits that have come about from the work done on the project. First, university and PDS faculty use the web to support technology-enhanced course offerings by using Blackboard and similar supports. Second, many of the faculty interns have engaged their students in the use of technology by requiring the development of electronic portfolios. Third, PDS faculty often selected to use multimedia software to enhance their teaching, using programs such as Geometer's Sketchpad, Children's Publishing Center, I-Movies in chemistry and biology as well as engaging in broad-based research on the Internet for social studies and history.

A Brief Look at Evaluation and Implications

Data were collected during the third year of the project to determine effectiveness. The evaluation was conducted by an external evaluator with support from two project employees. Data were collected by examining information from a number of different sources. These included: (a) pre- and post- technology skills assessment, (b) intern and mentor feedback, (c) project planning documents, (d) logs of project meetings, (e) observations of classroom visits, and, (f)) reflective summaries. Interns and mentors were required to gather data and to complete several different forms and surveys about their work on the project. Quantitative and qualitative methods were used to analyze the data.

The first series of data analyses performed was on the skills that the interns gained from participanting in the project. T-tests were conducted to determine significant changes in skills. Interns significantly enhanced their technology skills on 12 of 21 items assessed (with significance at least at the .05 level). Project staff independently rated seven of these items as vital skills to be learned by participating in the project. These skills include: general computing, word processing, Internet use, use of e-mail, online instruction, presentation of instructional materials, and the design of web page software. In addition, interns demonstrated significant improvements in their use of Windows operating systems, computing graphics, assistive technologies, digital cameras, and scanners.

Data were collected to determine changes in the instructional practices of the interns. Positive changes were noted in 12 of the 14 items analyzed. Important instructional changes included the selection of appropriate digital content, use of technology to differentiate instruction, transfer of knowledge to students through modeling technology integration, locating and evaluating web projects, and developing original, interactive digital projects.

In addition data were analyzed about the instructional impact of the integration project. All of the interns indicated their work in the project would have an immediate instructional impact. For the mentors, the majority (82.6%) indicated there would be an immediate instructional impact.

The support provided by mentors to interns was rated as well. More than three fourths of the respondents (77.3%) found the support provided to be extremely helpful, and close to an additional one fifth of the respondents (18.2%) indicated support was very important. These results are indicative of the mentor model being an effective means of assisting in integrating technology with one's instructional practices. In terms of overall satisfaction with the mentor program, mentors and interns were asked to rate their experience. Mentors and interns (22 out of 23 participants or 95.7%) rated the program as being excellent or very good.

Program Impact

During the first two years of the project, *more than 700 pre-service* teachers participated in grant activities. By the end of the third year, over 950 pre-service teachers participated, and by the end of the fourth year an additional 32 pairs of teachers in PDS sites and over 75% of the full-time faculty in the College of Education were involved as either a mentor or intern.

There were unanticipated benefits. Faculty who completed the project noted growth on a number of levels. First, when asked: "In reflecting on your experience as a mentor or intern, what has been its greatest benefit to you?" One participant stated, "I had an opportunity to collaborate in a cross-curricular way with another staff person. Together we created a project that I feel will benefit the students' understanding of the content." This statement underlines a core goal of improving students' content knowledge.

Second, a school media specialist and teacher who served as a mentor for three years working with three different interns commented, "What I realized as I began working with my first intern that was she and I were actually collaborating. We developed classroom projects that fit her curriculum, but I gained a better understanding of that grade level curriculum, which, in turn, benefited my program, as well. I became excited about cross-curricular projects we could plan and implement together, using aspects of the language arts and technology curriculum in conjunction with the media curriculum. As a result of that experience, I realized that this program doesn't just teach one person about using computers. This project builds a bridge between two staff members, which then filters outward."

This project was successful in helping teachers to integrate technology into their teaching. For instance, teachers from the same PDS site had opportunities to collaborate at times of the day convenient for them. In addition, providing rewards and support to these pairs of teachers working in a PDS site was also related to project success. The stipend was a reward for intensive work accomplished on site and was relevant to the instruction occurring at that site.

Another successful element of the project was the use of the mentor model at the PDS site that could be observed as occurring in the natural environment of the school by other teachers and teacher candidates. The effectiveness of the mentor model and the work accomplished by mentors and interns was reinforced when demonstrated to the rest of the PDS school community during the project showcase convened in mid-Spring. In addition, each pair was given access to computers and a range of digital devices to facilitate a gallery walk event for Towson University faculty.

Summary

This project has been effective in supporting teacher education and the professional development of faculty within the Towson PDS Network. The collaboration between the university and partner schools is compelling just as the relationship has been between the mentor and intern. Through the work done in collaboration, eventually technology becomes part of the teaching and learning paradigm. At the same time, student learning is extended to include the computer, digital camera, presentation software, and other media resources. These are all important tools in a twenty-first century learning environment, and now more universally recognized by a range of teachers in our PDS sites.

References

Holland, P. E. (2001). Professional development in technology: Catalyst for school reform. *Journal of Technology and Teacher Education, 9*, 245–267.

Kariuki, M., Franklin, T., & Duran, M. (2001). A technology partnership: Lessons learned by partners. *Journal of Technology and Teacher Education, 9*, 407–417.

Kerka, S. (1998). New perspectives on mentoring. (ERIC Digest No. 194). Columbus, OH: ERIC Clearinghouse on Adult Career and Vocational Education. (ERIC Document Reproduction Service No. ED418249)

MacArthur, C. A., Pilato, V., Kercher, M., Peterson, D., Malouf, D., & Jamison, P. (1995). Mentoring: An approach to technology education for teachers. *Journal of Research on Computing in Education, 28,* 46–62.

Sprague, D., Kopfman, K., & Dorsey, S. (1998). Faculty development in the integration of technology in teacher education courses. *Journal of Computing in Teacher Education, 14,* 24–28.

Wheeler, E. J., Wilson, G. P., & Berkeley, T. R. (2001). Bringing web-enhanced courses to communities of learners in early childhood education. *Journal of Early Childhood Teacher Education, 22,* 237–242.

PART FOUR

Standards and Sustainability

CHAPTER TEN

The NCATE Professional Development School Standards Field Test Project

Jane E. Neapolitan & Chet Scott

Introduction

When the idea of a professional development school was first proposed to the principal of Owings Mills Elementary School in northwest Baltimore County, he could not imagine what might happen with the entire school staff. In 1994, Owings Mills Elementary School was a low-performing and diverse Title I school facing many challenges. Housed in its original 70-year-old building, the school had undergone several physical changes during its history in order to accommodate an increasing student population. However, the principal saw that a school with such challenges needed more than physical changes in order to help all students learn. The only way for there to be success would be to reinvent the school from *within*, and such a reinvention would require *the best teachers possible*. The idea of highly qualified master teachers working with teacher candidates (interns) in reflective practice provided an attractive new identity for the school and its staff.

The roles and responsibilities of teachers changed instantaneously. Instead of viewing themselves as teachers assigned to and responsible for a single classroom in a "tough school," they were teacher leaders, i.e., master teachers. In addition to teaching a given class of students in a given grade, they were responsible for creating and implementing a school plan in which the focus was on increased student achievement, the professional development of future teachers, and their own professional development. Changing the roles and responsibilities of the teachers validated them. Moreover, the personnel directly responsible for student achievement were endowed with ownership of the new effort. The teachers and staff could best articulate the needs of students as well as the challenges in their school, challenges with the curriculum, and the challenges associated with obtaining the professional development opportunities necessary to affect positive student achievement.

There was excitement throughout the school. Excitement, though, was not enough. The teachers and other staff needed strong leadership, a custom-designed professional development plan, and team-building experiences to create a unified staff with a shared vision, mission, and agreed-upon strategic plan. The PDS model effectively and efficiently provided the resources teachers needed to perform their new roles and responsibilities. The collaboration between the university and the schoolhouse was mutually beneficial. The university provided an additional perspective, tailor-made professional development and increased roles and responsibilities for teachers. The schoolhouse provided a real-world internship for teacher candidates. In turn, the schoolhouse helped to refine and revolutionize the internship, providing graduates with a more substantive experience and insuring cadres of teachers qualified and prepared to teach in challenging schools. For the first time ever, the university and the school worked collaboratively, rather than separately, in the continual design and implementation of teacher preparation and the professional development of experienced professionals.

Given this premise, staff members at Owings Mills Elementary School had to make a decision about their future. The school was given permission to interview current staff who wished to remain at the school as well as new staff from other schools and districts. Each staff member had to agree to participate in reflective practice including intensive professional development, performance assessment/action research, and the mentoring of interns. As a result of this dramatic internal change, in 1994 the school was reborn as the first Towson University Professional Development School.

As the principal and new staff set about the mission of creating a community of learners, they did not realize they were breaking new ground for teacher professionalism. The university provided a weeklong strategic planning institute for teachers and parents that resulted in the Owings Mills/Towson University Professional Development School. Participants identified the critical components of a model school to create a shared vision, mission, and action plan. The action plan was a "living" document in which a course of action was outlined that the staff would implement throughout the year. Teachers were identified in the plan to provide leadership for all initiatives. They created three action teams to drive the implementation of the school plan in terms of student achievement/staff development, a safe and nurturing environment, and community outreach. All former committees were disbanded resulting in the coordination of the vision, mission, and goals of the school plan.

Part of the groundbreaking exchange between the university and the school was bringing 16 interns to the school from the Elementary Education Department at Towson University. These students volunteered to undergo their entire two-year professional education program (junior and senior years) in the new PDS setting. All of their professional courses were delivered at the PDS site in a dedicated classroom. The interns were immersed in the new culture of the partnership and became members of the school's staff. In short, the PDS was like a teaching hospital, providing the best connections between theory and practice for the improved learning of experienced educators and beginning teachers. In 1998, this collaborative "experiment" in teacher preparation brought acclaim to the partnership when cited as the "Outstanding Teacher Education Program" by the Association of Teacher Educators. The school focused all of its professional development energies on learning how to develop and implement performance-based assessments, and student scores on the Maryland School Performance Assessment Program (MSPAP) continued to improve.

The Development of Standards

In the years following the initial strategic planning institute, the focus was on student learning and increased student achievement. In 1995–1996, the partnership created a Network Coordinating Council with the Baltimore County Public Schools (BCPS). The network theme was a "Community of Learners," and its coordinating council included high-level personnel from the university, the school, and the school system. At monthly meetings (including the principal of the school, the dean of the College of Education, university professors, a specialist from the BCPS Staff Development Office, and classroom teacher representatives) members met to discuss strengths and needs of the partnership. All members had an equal voice. As a result of the meetings, many innovations evolved that were directly related to the success of the PDS concept. Council members recognized the need to identify additional partnerships as well as site coordinators (teachers who were paid a stipend to facilitate school-based PDS concerns) for each school in the network. The addition of partnerships resulted in greater synergy and facilitated the sharing of "best practices" among schools. Schools reported initiatives and jointly coordinated the use of resources to provide personnel with state-of-the-art professional development.

While the Towson University/Owings Mills Elementary School partnership continued its joint work, the PDS movement became a national phenomenon. School-university partnerships were designated to unite the functions of "professional preparation of [teacher] candidates, faculty development, inquiry directed at the improvement of practice, and enhanced student learning" (NCATE, 2001, p.1) became a national PDS focus. In order to ensure the quality of these partnerships, the National Council for Accreditation of Teacher Education (NCATE) conducted a national project to field test Standards for Professional Development Schools (1998–2001). The Towson University/Owings Mills Professional Development School partnership seized the opportunity and applied to be a part of the NCATE project as the next step in its development.

In 1998, Towson University/Owings Mills PDS was one of 20 partnerships selected to participate in an intensive and extensive process of self-examination, reflection, and inquiry that would point the way for its future growth and development. The balance of this chapter is a description of the school's participation in the NCATE PDS Standards Field Test Project and the "lessons learned" from the self-study and site visit by a national team of experts. In addition, the project's validation is discussed with focus on what was known intuitively about the partnership, i.e., its strength is in the outstanding quality of the collaboration and meeting the learning needs of its members.

The Self-Study

The self-study documented the history of the partnership and provided a process for reflecting on the partnership's development. Several meetings and seminars provided by NCATE and the university gave partnership members an orientation to the PDS Draft Standards (Levine, 1998). The draft standards focused on five "Critical Attributes of a PDS": (a) the Learning Community, (b) Collaboration, (c) Accountability and Quality Assurance, (d) Organization, Roles, and Structures, and (e) Equity and Diversity. The functions and critical attributes of the PDS set forth by NCATE were similar to the functions and goals set forth by the Towson University/Baltimore County Public Schools PDS Network: (a) Collaboration, (b) Enhanced Pre-service

Teacher Education, (c) Continuing Professional Development, (d) Inquiry, (e) Student Achievement, and (f) Dissemination of Promising Practices.

A Partnership Steering Committee was formed with representation from the school, the university, and the school system. A 25-page self-study report was written describing the development, innovations, and accomplishments of the partnership in its brief four-year history.

As a learning community, several efforts and activities were reinforced in considering the learning of all members. First, through continuous professional development in the school and throughout the network, teachers took on new roles and responsibilities. In turn, children were able to learn in a safe and nurturing environment, and a school that was once "tough" demonstrated its ability to increase its performance on the state assessment. Second, members of the learning community took joint responsibility for the preparation of the pre-service interns. For example, a team of school, university, and school system personnel worked together (for a year) in developing a performance-based assessment for pre-service teachers based on the standards of the Interstate New Teacher Assessment and Support Consortium (INTASC). The development and implementation of the performance assessment was a notable accomplishment, bringing together the functions of continuing professional development and teacher preparation.

Third, the university wrote and received several grants, including a Goals 2000 grant and an Eisenhower Grant enabling continued collaboration. One of the highlights of the collaboration was the creation of a new PDS instructional facilitator position jointly funded between the university and the school system. The "boundary spanner's" role included university teaching, P–12 staff development, interorganizational communication and coordination, and assessment coordination. The partnership held that the PDS instructional facilitator's role successfully influenced change by linking the cultures of the school and the university.

Fourth, accountability and quality assurance in the PDS were predicated on standards used to frame the teacher preparation program. These included standards from INTASC, the National Council of Teachers of Mathematics (NCTM), as well as the Essential Dimensions of Teaching (EDOT, the Maryland INTASC equivalent). The performance-based assessment of pre-service teachers was based on a three-part system for the evaluation of interns. The system included the use of a formative observational instrument with specific outcomes and indicators, a summative assessment form, and the development and evaluation of a professional portfolio. The system provided consensus on what interns should know and be able to do and also a vehicle for stimulating dialogue about what constitutes quality teaching.

Fifth, new structures such as the Network Coordinating Council and new roles such as the PDS instructional facilitator helped support the organization of the partnership. Pooled monetary resources from grants and operating budgets allowed for benefits to accrue to all members of the partnership. These included assigned time to work on the development and implementation of the PDS for university faculty, stipends for mentor teachers, site liaisons, and for interns to attend start-of-school days in August. Funds also supported participation in national and local conferences, including attendance at planning retreats. Inclusion of the interns in these activities provided an additional human resource in the PDS. Interns participated in a number of service projects including providing child care at Parents' Night programs and producing a memory book with photos of all the school's children.

And, sixth, Owings Mills Elementary School is a very diverse school. Continuing professional development activities, including a graduate course in "Teaching in a Multicultural/Multiethnic Society" and "Gender Equity" workshops presented by David Sadker, provided opportunities for teachers to increase their knowledge and skills in teaching a diverse student population. Interns learned about the needs of different learners by tutoring, assisting teachers and parents in the "Terrific Kids Program," and conducting a "Multicultural Night." Overall, the self-study and other inquiry revealed the partnership had created a community of learners.

The Inquiry Project

The overarching goal of the inquiry project was to demonstrate the connections between the four functions of PDS: teacher preparation, professional development, inquiry, and student achievement. A Towson University faculty member was assigned as the research liaison, while a former PDS coordinator and current assistant principal district mentor teacher facilitated the project's logistics.

"Tying Together Teacher Education and Student Learning," was an examination of how some of the partnership's performance assessment activities impacted children, student teachers, and mentor teachers in the school. According to Teitel (2000), impact research on specific outcomes of PDSs has not been widely conducted. This is due, in part, to the fact that most PDS research has relied on data from surveys and other methods that only scratch the surface of this kind of effort. With the support of NCATE, the inquiry project would be deeper and more complex than any other research previously conducted in the partnership. The inquiry would focus on the *understanding* of performance assessment and less on the technical aspects of it.

Three questions guided the inquiry project:

1. What is the level of understanding about performance assessment held by teacher candidates in a performance- and standards-based teacher preparation program in a PDS?
2. In what ways does collaboration on performance assessment and instruction affect the knowledge, skills, and attitudes (KSAs) of mentor teachers and teacher candidates?
3. What are the effects on students of collaboration by mentor teachers and teacher candidates on performance assessment and instruction?

Participants consisted of three convenience samples selected in Spring 2000. These included 15 undergraduate interns (white females, ages 20 to 35), five mentor teachers (two minority females and three white females with a range of 10 to 20 years teaching experience), five students from Grade 3 (three minority males, one minority female, and one white female), and four students from Grade 5 (one white male, two minority females and one white female). This was a microethnographic study in which multiple and varied sources of data for qualitative analyses were used. The methods included, for example, interns' written reflections on their student teaching experiences, mentor teachers' written reflections on their collaboration with the interns, and performance assessments designed and implemented by the interns and their mentor teachers. Other sources of data included transcripts of focus groups with interns, mentor teachers, and children in which they discussed their understandings of performance assessment.

A total of 276 documents for the project were digitally scanned and subjected to qualitative analysis using QSR NUD*IST 4 software. The transcripts of focus groups were returned to the participants to be reviewed for omissions and biases. The transcripts were subjected to expert review by teachers and university faculty outside the partnership. Samples of performance assessments created by interns at Owings Mills Elementary School and by interns at a Towson non-PDS student teaching center were subjected to blind review by a state expert. Analysis of the documents yielded 2,122 coded units used to create the categories for the findings. The inquiry project was limited because it was a case study that used intact groups and was conducted by a participant-observer. Also, it was limited by the small number of participants in the study. However, the implications drawn from the study can be applied to other cohorts of teacher candidates and to mentor teachers and children in similar PDSs.

Findings from the data suggested that interns developed their understandings of performance assessment through *co-learning* experiences with other interns, mentor teachers, university professors, and children. The strong emphasis on staff development at the school for designing and implementing performance assessments was clear. The interns viewed their learning as metacognition in which they were "weaned from their teachers" in order to perform independently. They understood why they implemented certain technical aspects of performance assessment and related those "whys" to broader issues of instruction, classroom management, and developing a personal teaching style. For the interns, the underlying impetus for these understandings was the preparation of children to perform well on the state assessment program. An independent evaluator concluded that performance assessments co-created by interns and mentors at the school were of a higher technical quality than those created by individuals. Once again, it was clear that the intensive and extensive co-learning experiences for interns and mentors had yielded higher quality products.

Mentor teachers had a slightly different understanding of performance assessment than did their less-experienced intern partners. Although they praised the process of learning how to use performance assessment side by side with interns, they did not focus as much on technical aspects. Instead, mentor teachers were more concerned about learner differences when using performance assessments. The mentors, master teachers, analyzed their experience with performance assessments more critically with the objective of helping *all* children learn. In addition, mentor teachers were concerned about the resources needed to implement performance assessments. Obtaining and purchasing materials, e.g., to make pancakes or carve pumpkins, required resources that went beyond typical school supplies. Finally, mentor teachers took ownership of learning how to use performance assessments. They felt responsible for the "real world" effects of assessment on their students, especially children from diverse backgrounds and other special needs.

The NCATE inquiry project suggested there was an interdependency of learning within and among the three groups of mentor teachers, teacher candidates, and students at the school. Interns (referred to by the children as "the Towson teachers") enabled the students to recover their learning through one-on-one assistance in classrooms. Students, like their adult counterparts in the school, learned that if they "messed up" they would be given multiple opportunities to re-learn and re-do important information and skills. Thus, there was substantial evidence that a synergy existed between the high level of collaboration and learning at Owings Mills Elementary School. The question remained, however, as to what resources would sustain the synergy, especially in a context of diverse learners.

The Site Visit

A site visit took place between October 22–25, 2000. It was conducted in conjunction with Towson University's Initial Accreditation Visit by NCATE, and it was one of three such combined visits in the PDS Standards Field Test Project (NCATE, 2000, p. 3). The five-member PDS visit team included a university faculty member, an elementary classroom teacher, a middle school PDS faculty liaison, a college of education dean, and a project staff member. A Maryland State Department of Education member, who had received permission from the partnership, also joined the team as a "participant observer." All team members had extensive experience working with PDSs, and several had participated in other pilot site visits.

The visit was fashioned after the process used for NCATE accreditation visits and began with a formal presentation by the partnership at a local hotel on Sunday afternoon and a dinner on Sunday night. In order to prepare for the visit to the school on Monday and Tuesday, the team gathered and reviewed numerous artifacts supporting the specifications of the partnership in the self-study document. These artifacts included minutes of meetings, job descriptions, research reports, syllabi from pre-service and in-service education courses, faculty/intern handbooks, and state and district curriculum guides.

On Monday, it was clear team members were familiar with the various details of the history and development of the partnership. Team members asked strategic questions during interviews and focus group discussions to obtain a more thorough understanding of the PDS, and the visit assisted partnership members to reflect more deeply on where the partnership might be headed in the future. During the visit, team members made numerous observations of classrooms, attended an intern seminar, and interviewed teachers, school administrators, past and present interns, and university faculty and administrators. On the last day of the visit, team members deliberated about what they had read and seen and then reported their results.

The most important commendation given by NCATE was "the partnership has served as a lever for change in the educational reform movement at both the school and university level and as a model for PDS development in the larger professional community locally, regionally, and nationally" (NCATE, 2000, p. 18). The partnership was also commended for its serious and sustained attention to learning by all its members and its strong commitment to meeting the learning needs of all students. It was recommended that the partnership should "consider developing a partnership-wide vision of what a *collegial* program of inquiry and action research should involve as well as how participants could use their skills to implement such a program. This might involve thinking of inquiry as group deliberation on problems of practice focused on achievement test scores and teaching strategies, examination of student work, or the improvement of mentoring strategies for interns" (NCATE, 2000, p.18). Also, it was recommended that the partnership put in place an infrastructure to ensure better communication and dialogue for all stakeholder groups. Finally, it was recommended that the partnership should "find ways to highlight and celebrate its diversity in the PDS and its community" (NCATE, 2000, p. 19).

Sustaining Synergy by Utilizing Resources from Within

The Towson University/Owings Mills Professional Development School partnership in 2004 celebrates its tenth anniversary with the publication of this book. Over the years, there have been changes in the curriculum and the state assessment program, a lengthy renovation of the school building, stepping up the pace for a one-year internship for teacher candidates, and several turnovers in university staff. One constant factor, however, has been the leadership of the principal, which is a force for guiding the school's directions for the future as a PDS. The NCATE recommendations have resulted in a more deliberate and visible celebration of the diversity of the school. Service learning projects planned and carried out by interns and action research conducted by the interns now are aligned with the School Improvement Plan.

A new infrastructure for improving communication within the PDS has been established. Monthly coordinating council meetings during school hours have helped advance teacher leadership by giving mentor teachers more decision-making power about the internship. All mentor teachers now participate as examiners for the teacher candidates' portfolio reviews at midpoint and at the end of the internship year. Teachers continue to earn graduate credit by taking courses delivered on site and at a reduced rate through the Towson Learning Network (TLN). Although external funding resources are not as plentiful as in the early days of the partnership, the PDS continues to develop as a community of learners. In a "mature" partnership, a "knowledge capital" has been developed during the past decade. This has become a new and important resource for sustaining the synergy of the PDS into its future.

The PDS has confirmed the belief as well as providing a collective experience that there is a synergy between collaboration and learning. Concerning the future, continuing to find more effective ways of accessing and allocating the resources of "time, space, people, and money" (NCTAF, 1996) in order to sustain synergy is important. At a time of scarce monetary resources and higher standards of accountability, partnership members must · look *within* to glean the best talent, the deepest meanings, and the most important directions for the PDS to continue to grow.

References

Levine, M. (Ed.) (1998). *Designing standards that work for professional development schools.* Washington, DC: National Council for Accreditation of Teacher Education.

National Commission on Teaching & America's Future (1996). *What matters most: Teaching for America's future.* New York: Author.

National Council for Accreditation of Teacher Education (2000, October). *Site visit report. NCATE professional development school draft standards pilot project.* Washington, DC: Author.

National Council for Accreditation of Teacher Education (2001). *Standards for professional development schools.* Washington, DC: Author.

Teitel, L. (2000). *Assessing the impacts of professional development schools.* Washington, DC: American Association of Colleges of Teacher Education.

Afterword

Terry R. Berkeley with Pamela W. Morgan

Above the front entrance to the United States National Archives engraved in large block letters for all who enter seeking to see the nation's written documents and the heritage of our unique American democracy are the words: "The Past Is Prologue." The contributors to this book have combined their thoughts in a community effort to produce a prologue on Towson University's perspective of the professional development school. We have done so because of a shared caring for that which we do best: prepare new teachers and offer advanced work to practicing professional educators, all of us having in our minds the learning of children in public schools. Notably, these efforts are accomplished in partnership with personnel from the Maryland State Department of Education, our colleagues in local school district central offices, and in concert with teachers, staff, and administrators in community public schools. Yet there is a need for a starting place for all of this activity described in the chapters preceding this Afterword. Therefore, we begin with the ideal Plato suggests in, *The Republic* that in a Republic nothing can be more important than the care and nurturing of the young. For educators, especially, can there be anything more important than moving toward this ideal?

Summing up the work of the authors of this book and finding a way to bring together the cohesive values of community and caring, ideals discussed in the Foreword, have been provocative and honor filled. The authors have offered a richness of material, providing an interesting combination of themes about which to write further and to work further, and they have allowed a certain faith that the Afterword would be reflective of their ideas and efforts. The co-editors trust that the road all of us travel will in some way be viewed with a particular professional allegiance and dedication to public schooling and the art and craft of working with teachers, new and practicing.

Community and caring are evocative of people and place. There is no doubt that a professional development school partnership consists of many people in many places. To be successful, the PDS must be a caring enterprise located in the place of a school, in the place of a university, each located in a community or a part of the community, inter-connected, even if considered or treated in isolation. To be sure, Bronfenbrenner (1979) has much to say in a similar vein about this kind of ecology of development: human and organizational, as people and place are at a nexus in moving toward more advanced states of understanding in all of their activity.

How might the importance of place (the places of the PDS partners) be described? Turning to literature, Eudora Welty (1954, 1990) asked, "What place has place in fiction?" In each of the replies to herself, to us, Welty weaves people into place, "because the novel from the start has been bound up in the local, the real, the present, the ordinary day-to-day of human experience. Where the imagination comes in is in directing the use of all this." (p. 1)

The imagination of the PDS is made real by the players, the central characters located in the place of school and university and community. The imagination of the PDS is made real by the bringing together of resources, dilemmas, joys, elations, the contradictions of two cultures creating a third, the PDS itself, and within a fourth, the larger context of the broader local community

The PDS is complex. It moves "out there" and it moves within itself. To engage in PDS work means one goes beyond what is usual. It means one takes risks; it means one lives in ways that are consuming. It means one is committed to change and understanding the "mystery" of that change or at least learning to understand that mystery. It is easy to understand, then, that the PDS, indeed, is a community of learners.

What did the authors of the chapters offer to indicate this new form of community? What themes did the authors point to indicating the risks they take now toward a new and more progressive future for the ultimate beneficiaries of schooling, children?

Themes

Respecting Change, Respectful Change

Throughout the preceding chapters, change—systemic change—among individuals and groups of people has been described. Therefore, the "condition" of teacher preparation and the professional development of practicing professional educators *before* the creation of the PDS has not been as effective as it might have been. As with any exploration, risks and fits and starts are associated in changing a former state-of-affairs into a new efficient and respectful model of teaching and learning. In an era of constant calls for data pointing to immediate positive effects, especially in terms of the impact upon the learning of students in schools, the results of change in teacher preparation and the professional development of practicing professional educators had to be known almost before the shift in approach was designed and implemented. Further, all of the partners to PDS partnerships were interested in the success of the efforts in which they were engaged and in which they had put so much energy. This was made to be even a more significant goal because two years or so after the first PDS partnerships began at Towson, the State of Maryland required that by 2004 all students engaging in a teacher training program had to receive their training in a professional development school.

Inevitably this was an endeavor of merging communities into a better approach, a paradigm shift, if you will, with an investment or buy-in of the central figures, the players, being essential. Think for a moment of school people being provided with greater autonomy in matters related to what was happening in their schools, the PDS itself, as well as their own professional development and in giving voice to the dynamics of a university's teacher preparation program. Think of university faculty and administrators moving outside of the safety and confines of teaching and reward systems traditional to life on campus. The establishment of a PDS, and, in turn, the establishment of a broader PDS network represent change in institutions and among individuals. Learning how to do all of this comfortably has taken time and patience, courage and investment, risk and commitment. Teachers as described are participating in shared governance in each PDS partnership and have an influence on the teacher preparation curricula in each College of Education department. University faculty members have undertaken changed roles—spending much of their time in schools, teaching and supervising students, participating as members of the school staff, and engaging in a reward system in the College at which their efforts are appreciated and encouraged and advocated for throughout campus.

Numerous examples of systemic change are described throughout the text as occurring in a number of communities, in numerous schools located in several school systems at different grade levels interwoven with the context of a university and vice versa. Almost indirectly, it seems, support for transformation is mentioned. Yet, the pith, the grit of daily PDS activity, is difficult to feel in a tangible way from a mere set of descriptions of what has happened during the past 10 years. Nevertheless, great change has taken place, and there is a feeling each participant has experienced that is a part of their being.

PDS work is labor intensive, requiring understanding and a constant belief and stewardship in the partnership and among individuals for success to occur. From two distinct cultures, one synergistic entity has had to emerge for each of the partnerships to be forged. Thus similar to what Clarke, Tarule, & Hood (1994) learned in their efforts in Vermont in school restructuring, change had to be top down and bottom up, as "together, university and school people [began] to both enact and understand a new form of collaboration. Abandoning earlier models of simple cooperation, theirs becomes a relationship in which vision can be shared, options can be negotiated, and new experiments can be designed....They may also uncover the sources of their own wisdom and expertise" (p. 292).

Diversity

As change has come to the schools and the university in the development of PDS partnerships and their relationships with one another, Maryland as a state has been undergoing intense demographic change during the previous 15 to 20 years. Diversity of all types has had to be learned intimately by PDS partners, most especially by university interns who found themselves in places and with people with whom they were often unfamiliar. For example, this was more complex than just learning about one or two or three groups in one place, as there were school partners where 20 or 30 or more languages were spoken in their classrooms with great variability in customs, traditions, and socioeconomic statuses among those speaking the same languages.

At the core in developing each network PDS partnership an important ingredient has been assuring a significant level of diversity from which interns could learn to work successfully with today's population of school students. In addition, interns have had to learn about the communities in which these schools are located and learn ways to repay to those communities for the opportunities provided to them to pursue their education in those places. Speak about synergy, acculturating students into new highly diverse places and then giving back to those places required a change in traditions and a transformation in understanding of those undergoing incredible developmental change in their journey of becoming educational professionals—teachers!

One might wonder if learning deeply about diversity is a unique undertaking. The answer to this query is "No. " What makes the Towson experience different? Perhaps the answer begins with the long previous experience of the university's students and faculty being and remaining just past the edge of an urban environment, feeling a safety in being part of a suburb. Next, and quite importantly, there has been leadership at all levels of the university advocating for an understanding of difference in a higher education community that has begun to change in not so subtle ways. In fact, the change in understanding of difference began slowly and picked up speed and scope once the PDS became an integral part of the university's teacher preparation programs.

In the 1978 case decided by the U.S. Supreme Court, *Regents of the University of California v. Bakke,* Justice Harry Blackmun wrote, "In order to get beyond racism, we must first take into account race." This is transformative work. In the transformation discussed here, it is not racism that had to be overcome but a lack of understanding, limits on experience, and great naiveté. In place of these characteristics has come understanding of others, competence in teaching a range of students from a range of backgrounds with a range of abilities, as well as understanding about and involvement in the community. Oakes & Lipton (2004) borrow from W.E.B. DuBois (1935) as they discuss this kind of change:

> The proper education of any people includes sympathetic touch between teacher and pupil; knowledge on the part of the teachers, not simply the individual taught, but of his surroundings and background, and the history of his class and group; such contact between pupils, and between teacher and pupil, on the basis of perfect social equality, as will increase this sympathy and knowledge. (p. vii)

No other statement, it seems, provokes to a greater degree the need for attending to diversity and its complexities than the impact of the important relationship between a teacher and students, especially on issues related to social justice and equality. Also, "sympathetic touch" is as poignant a symbol as there can be of caring and community, people and place.

On being a minority within a minority. In the past, the relationship between the university and the schools in the professional preparation of teachers and the professional development of practicing educational professionals has been merely collaborative. Some of these relationships to be sure were respectful, caring, and close. Rarely, though, did school personnel spend significant time at the university, and even more rarely did university personnel spend time in the school as a member of the school community (not as a researcher). The boundary spanner role of the instructional facilitator addressed this rarity by creating the opportunity for an educator to walk in both worlds—the public school world and the higher education world—simultaneously.

This rarity presented new challenges and realities that intensified when the person who walked in both worlds was a person of color, a minority within a minority. In the public school world, she was a higher education person, while, at the same time, a public school person in the higher education world, and frequently the sole source and voice of diversity in both worlds. In stark contrast there were times when the boundary spanner was looked upon as the person of color representing a "white" institution and utilizing talents that would better benefit people who looked like her, preferably at a historically black institution. Consequently, a subtle drama, a sub-plot if you will, was evolving, often unnoticed, within the PDS initiative, in much the same way as the play within the play was crafted in Shakespeare's *A Midsummer Night's Dream*. While many individuals within the network were oblivious to its existence, the person of color was very much aware of the unfolding drama with its tensions and discomfort.

From the inside looking out, the boundary-spanning role offered opportunities to demonstrate a wealth of knowledge and expertise in two different worlds while gaining additional experiences that enhanced that expertise. Unfortunately, deeply rooted, systemic attitudes and perceptions about race and ethnicity often threatened opportunities to learn from and with someone who, while different, had much to offer. In spite of possessing impressive credentials that made the boundary spanner highly qualified to do this work, her credibility had to be re-established over and over again. Once she recovered from the shock of the way things still were and recognized that a greater cause was being served—paving the way—the challenge to persist became even more important to accept.

There is an interesting and unique situation. Because of the transformative nature of the PDS with the dilemma of a conflict within a drama—education and example—many of the education majors in the network as discussed in these chapters had to take a prerequisite course on "Teaching and Learning in a Diverse Society." One outcome of the course has been students demonstrating "an appreciation for living and working in increasingly diverse local and global communities." Ideally, students emerge from this course eager to improve achievement for every learner; however, the environments in which they practice and hone their craft tend to reflect institutionalized attitudes and perceptions regarding issues of equity and diversity. In challenging the status quo, Delpit (1995) suggests, "we must learn to be vulnerable enough to allow our world to turn upside down in order to allow the realities of others to edge themselves into our consciousness" (p. 47). Also, according to Lieberman and Miller (1999), efforts need to be to created, "new learning communities [that] include rather than exclude, that create knowledge rather than merely apply it, and that offer challenge and support; [such communities] provide the greatest hope for [educators] who are in the process of transforming themselves, their world, and their work." (p. 91). Finally, the simplest of solutions resides in the poetry of a ten-year-old (who shall remain nameless) whose response to inequitable treatment was, "Treat me the way that I treat you—kindly."

Benefits of Collaboration

In the network, State of Maryland and NCATE standards are implemented with benefits accruing to each partner and stakeholder. The benefits of the work accomplished to date include significant collaboration between school and university personnel for the improved preparation of new teachers, for expanding professional development opportunities for professionals allowing for their continued growth and pride in the work they are doing as career educators, and for the positive impact upon students in the schools.

PDS accomplishments do not occur unless there is focus and energy directed at the steps leading to effective partnerships, efficient collaboration. The corollary notion or metaphor of "It takes a whole village to raise a PDS" is true. A PDS partnership, as discussed in each of the chapters, is the essence of collaboration among many people sharing jointly developed goals and objectives. The effort of moving to collaboration will go beyond the boundaries of schools, universities, and communities. Dettmer, Thurston, and Dyck (1993) note: "Collaboration is the future. It is intrinsic to school reform and restructuring, interagency cooperation, responses to changing student needs, and future global economic, demographic, and technological trends...[providing] a basis for continued collaboration throughout the global village" (p. 395).

Challenges

There are themes revolving about the ability of PDS partnerships to maintain their original intensity in teacher training, professional development, student achievement, and community involvement. As mentioned, PDS work is labor intensive for all of the partners. Though trite, perhaps, as with any other endeavor, success in the PDS only comes with zeal, diligence, and dedication to task. In and of itself, over time, this is an important challenge. Also, there are other real and formidable challenges to the PDS in obtaining resources, maintaining an excitement for PDS work ("sustainability"), the fit of the life and work of the PDS into No Child Left Behind legislation, and leadership.

Obtaining Resources

Until recently, there were state (e.g., Maryland State Department of Education, Maryland Higher Education Commission, and University System of Maryland) dollars and other resources available to support the establishment and on-going implementation of the PDS partnership. Given the economics of the times and the impact of No Child Left Behind, these available funds have been severely decreased or eliminated. In Maryland, the PDS initiative faces an uncertain funding future.

An examination of the PDS work done during the past 10 years has resulted in an approximate annual $9,500 cost of operating a professional development school partnership. This amount includes costs associated with strategic planning, professional development activities, collaborative activities, stipends for liaisons from the schools, stipends for teachers and other non-twelve-month school employees for participation in a variety of PDS activities, local travel, and materials and supplies. As can be seen, very few of these dollars go to university personnel with the exception of local travel costs, some conference travel, and some dollars for planning and engaging in professional development activities, and these are for faculty who are on 10-month contracts. For the first time, a percentage of these dollars has come from the university, and some funds come from fees charged to student interns who formerly had been charged for costs related to student teaching. In two or three cases, local school districts share in some of these expenses, providing stipends for liaisons and for participation in planning activities.

Afterword

Sustainability

While labor intensity is a challenge for maintaining the PDS partnership, greater issue seems to be the sustainability of the PDS. In this case, sustainability might be described as maintaining and continuing an excitement for the PDS partnership with a concomitant appreciation for and continuation of benefits for each partner and stakeholder. Sustainability is a positive attribute needing to be recognized because it exists.

From a Zen perspective, it is, or sustainability is. Sustainability is more than resilience in maintaining adherence to PDS goals and objectives, and, for lack of a better term, it is not "organizational endurance." Instead, sustainability requires a kind of getting into shape and being dedicated to working in a close partnership with people one has just met, whom one is learning to know more about, and finding out that even if you were not to get along in any other venue of life, there is appreciation for learning, sharing, caring, and community that adds value to the context of students in the schools, students from the university, and colleagues.

Orren (1990) suggests the kind of energy required of sustainability is that of going beyond self-interest. It may be that in education sustainability is mentioned so little in the literature because changes in the current state of the art are replaced by newer changes if new policy demands are to be met. Yet a search of "sustainability" on www.google.com results in 3.14 million possible hits (with attendant duplications) in just 0.13 seconds! While the majority of the sites explored focus on the sustainability of natural resources and efforts dedicated to sustaining those resources, universally it was noted that sustainability requires a shift in thinking to working in partnership, to considering on-going a dedication to task, and to maintaining dedicated effort to assure a greater good. These traits are at the heart and core of PDS partnerships.

No Child Left Behind

A major component of the No Child Left Behind Act is the professional development of practicing education professionals and paraprofessionals as well as the need for higher qualifications of new teachers in moving beyond merely being certified to becoming "Highly Qualified." The fit of the PDS partnership into No Child Left Behind at this point has not been specified in any detail. Yet, most importantly, there is nothing in No Child Left Behind

of the PDS into American schooling, and the ex-
...d objectives of the Towson PDS Network follow
...ectives of No Child Left Behind.

...preparation of teachers as described in this book will
...s to be certified and Highly Qualified in Maryland upon
...n. In PDS professional development activities, courses and other
...vities can lead current practicing professionals to become Highly Qualified, thus assisting these personnel in meeting this policy objective to provide great assurance to the parents and families of the students they teach.
Also, in addition, during Summer 2003, the first for-credit undergraduate
course was offered to PDS practicing paraprofessionals as they move to becoming Highly Qualified under the law.

As more and more data become available, adding to current data regarding the impact of PDS on students in schools and the best practices taught
and implemented through the PDS, the Towson Network will contribute its
own compendium of scientifically based research information, pointing to
the validity of the PDS in training new teachers and enhancing and adding to
the skills of practicing professionals. As mentioned previously, Towson is a
partner with the Maryland State Department of Education through the par-
tially state-supported Towson Institute for Professional Development School
Studies. Therefore, documenting the benefits of PDS efforts is a crucial vari-
able in all Towson PDS work, thus helping to sustain the efforts described in
this book. No Child Left Behind, then, is seen as an asset to the PDS partnership or, more importantly, as an opportunity to extend the network into the
future as the most efficient and effective means of preparing new teachers,
working with practicing teachers, and engaging in public schooling.

Leadership

For the PDS to yield positive benefits and effects for all stakeholders, leadership from each partner and among all partners is vital. As the PDS is a new
conceptual framework for school and university faculty members, it is a new
shift in outlook for principals, central office personnel, and university administrators, from department chairs, to deans, to the provost. Principals are
comfortable in operating their schools with independence (or as much independence as there can be in these times of stricter accountability), meeting
new central office priorities, and in being subject to more persistent public
scrutiny. Thus at a time when there are increased pressures on building ad-

ministrators, a more insistent call has come for collaboration and openness between two institutions that in the past have been reasonably well separated. Instead of being responsible for just the school, responsibility extends to shared responsibility for a partnership having the same dynamics as any other organizational entity. Concurrently, university faculty and administrators responsible for PDS partnerships are used to a kind of independence and freedom in the work they do. They, too, as has been described, have had to change how they approach their work.

One might use terms from human development (Meisels, 1979) to describe the important elements of organizational change or dynamics experienced as a result of PDS efforts that have an impact upon schools and the university, the efforts a leader must maintain if the partnership is to be sustained. The four critical elements of PDS development seem to revolve about (1) maturation, or change in the organization over time; (2) action in the physical world, or knowing and understanding the importance of place (school, community, and, then, university) in the development of the PDS; (3) interaction in the social world, or the constancy of interconnectedness among all of the stakeholders to the PDS as well as those observers of the PDS who are not members of the PDS in the immediate setting of school or university; and (4) equilibration or self-regulation, adapting to the demands of the complex environment of the PDS organization.

Closing Comment

In Vermont there is a belief in a human scale to democracy, government, participation, and leadership (Bryan and McClaughry, 1989). PDS partnerships as described are a reflection of a human scale to democracy. For example, even with the more overarching need to adhere to standards that are externally required (but on which local contributions were sought and included), the PDS is like a shire, a town or community council, reflective of the needs and requirements of those who are citizens of the shire that "begin with local powers kept exactly as they are until the people of the shire [e.g., PDS] vote to change them, they [then] will inherit a variety of ways of educational governance" (p. 187).

The Towson University PDS Network is like a collection of shires of citizens operating under similar principals, facing similar challenges, yet reflective of local needs and circumstances. As a result of the shire notion, there is legitimacy given to the implementation of externally required state and national PDS standards meaning there is a "street level effect" (Lipsky, 1983), whereby each individual entity interprets and, thus, re-draws policy to meet individual conditions and situations without changing the intent of the policy, in this case, standards guiding PDS activity. If the PDS is reflective of people and place, community and caring, as specified at the outset, rather than thinking of the PDS as an enfeebling of democracy, in fact, as Marris and Rein (1967, p. 7) suggest, this is the "triumph of democracy."

References

Bronfenbrenner, U. (1979). *The ecology of human development: Experiments by nature and design.* Cambridge, MA: Harvard University Press.

Bryan, F., & McClaughry. (1989). *The Vermont papers: Recreating democracy on a small scale.* Post Mills, VT: Chelsea Green.

Clarke, J. H., Tarule, J., & Hood, K. (1994). Schools and universities collaborate in development. In The Vermont Restructuring Collaborative (Ed.), *Field guide to educational renewal* (pp. 286-292). Brandon, VT: Holistic Education Press.

Delpit, L. (1995). *Other people's children: Cultural conflict in the classroom.* New York: The New Press.

Dettmer, P., Thurston, L.P.,& Dyck, N. (1993). *Consultation, collaboration, and teamwork: For students with special needs.* Boston: Allyn & Bacon.

DuBois, W.E.B. (1935). Does the Negro need separate schools? *Journal of Negro Education, 4*(3), 328.

Lieberman, A., & Miller, L. (1999). *Teachers—transforming their world and their work.* New York: Teachers College Press.

Lipsky, M. (1983). *Street-level bureaucracy: Dilemmas of the individual in public services.* New York: Russell Sage Foundation.

Marris, P., & Rein, M. (1967). *Dilemmas of social reform: Poverty and community action in the United States.* London: Routledge and Kegan Paul.

Meisels, S. J. (1979). *Special education and development: Perspectives on young children with special needs.* Baltimore: University Park Press.

Oakes, J. & Lipton, M. (2004). Foreword. In J. Romo, P. Bradfield, & R. Serrano, (Eds.), *Reclaiming democracy: Multicultural educators' journeys toward transformative teaching* (pp. vii–ix). Upper Saddle River, NJ: Pearson, Merrill Prentice Hall.

Orren, G. R. (1990). Beyond self-interest. In R.B. Reich (Ed.), *The power of public ideas.* Cambridge, MA: Harvard University Press.

University of California Bd. of Regents v. Bakke, 438 U.S. 265, 291 (1978).

Welty, E. (1954, 1990). *The eye of the story: Selected stories and reviews.* New York: Vintage Books.

Contributors

Joyce E. Agness is Project Facilitator for Least Restrictive Environment in the Department of Special Education, Howard County Public School System (MD). She received a B.A. from the University of Akron (1977); an M.A. in Special Education from Johns Hopkins University (1995); and an Ed.S. in Early Childhood Special Education from The George Washington University (2003).

Bess Altwerger is Professor of Elementary Education at Towson University. She teaches courses in and has published widely in the area of literacy development and instruction. Her recent research has focused on the impact of various reading programs on children's reading strategies and comprehension. She is currently working on her forthcoming book, *Reading for Profit: The Commercialization of Reading Instruction.*

Terry R. Berkeley is Professor and Chair of the Department of Early Childhood Education at Towson University, where he has developed numerous partnerships. These partnerships are an outgrowth of his doctoral work at Harvard University, his university teaching, and local service, which all focus on the building of community. He is co-editor of *Ensuring Safe School Environments: Exploring Issues, Seeking Solutions* (2003).

James B. Binko is Professor Emeritus at Towson University. During his forty-plus-year career at the university, he has held many positions, including Professor of Secondary Education and Dean of the College of Education. He has co-authored four books and numerous articles. In 1999, he was named Outstanding Geography Educator by the National Geographic Society.

Gregory Bryant is Chair of the Elementary Education Department at Towson University. A faculty member since 1990, he has been primarily involved with student teachers. Since 1997, he has been actively involved in the development of the department's professional development school initiatives, including developing new PDS sites.

Lynn C. Cole is Associate Professor of Elementary Education at Towson University and holds a Ph.D. in Reading Education from the University of Maryland, College Park. She has served as a classroom teacher and as state specialist in Gifted Education Programs for the Maryland State Department of Education. She currently works with professional development schools in the Howard County (MD) Public Schools.

Ann M. Eustis holds a B.A. (1983) from Wesleyan University in government and worked in legal research at the U.S. Department of Justice's Civil Rights Division. She also holds an M.Ed. from the University of Maryland and taught for 10 years in Prince George's County and Howard County (MD) public schools. At present, she is a PDS Site Coordinator for the Howard County Public School System.

Teresa T. Field is Assistant Professor at Johns Hopkins University in the Department of Teacher Preparation. She coordinates the development of Professional Development School partnerships with Baltimore City (MD) Public Schools. Her research focuses on teacher reflection and school reform efforts, such as technology infusion, data-driven instruction, and professional development schools.

Debi Gartland is Professor of Special Education at Towson University. She received a B.S.E. (1978) in Elementary Education and Special Education at Westfield State College (MA); an M.Ed. (1982) in Educational Administration/Special Education from Massachusetts College of Liberal Arts; and a Ph.D. (1986) in Special Education from The Pennsylvania State University.

Lisa Joy Greenberg has served at Owings Mills (MD) Elementary School since 1988, as a classroom teacher and currently as guidance counselor. She earned a B.S. in Elementary Education from Towson University and a Master's degree from Loyola College (Baltimore) in School Counseling.

Cynthia Hartzler-Miller earned her doctorate at Michigan State University. In addition to serving as Towson University's liaison to the Bel Air (MD) Professional Development School, she teaches undergraduate and graduate courses in social studies curriculum and instruction, educational policy, and the social contexts of schooling. Her research interests include teachers' subject matter knowledge, teacher change, and critical pedagogy.

Shelly S. Huggins is Assistant Professor in the Elementary Education Department at Towson University. She holds an Ed.D. from Morgan State University (2000) in Urban Educational Leadership. She served in the Baltimore County (MD) public schools in roles such as a math/science teacher, academic administrator, and reading specialist.

Todd Kenreich is Assistant Professor of Secondary Education at Towson University. As a university liaison, he works with high school/middle school partnerships in Baltimore County (MD) and Howard County (MD). He earned a bachelor's degree in government from Georgetown University and a master's and doctoral degree in social studies and global education from The Ohio State University.

Nechie Rochel King earned an M.Ed. from Harvard University and a Ph.D. from the University of Wisconsin-Madison. She has been teaching in the Elementary Education Department at Towson University since 1991.

Maggie Madden is a Program Approval Specialist for Teacher Preparation Programs and Coordinator of the Maryland Professional Development School Network at the Maryland State Department of Education. She is currently finishing her doctoral dissertation on the lived experience of university faculty in professional development schools.

Sally J. McNelis was the first Professional Development School Facilitator for the Secondary Education Department at Towson University. She taught in area public schools for 33 years and was the 1994–1995 Baltimore County Teacher of the Year.

Pamela Williams Morgan is Visiting Assistant Professor in Elementary Education at Towson University. Previously, she taught English/Language Arts for 22 years and then served as Instructional Facilitator in the Baltimore County (MD) PDS Network. She received the Milken Family Foundation National Educator Award in 1997 and the Towson University Excellence in Teacher Education Award in 2003.

Jane E. Neapolitan is Assistant Professor in the Elementary Education Department at Towson University. She earned an Ed.D. in Curriculum and Teaching from Teachers College, Columbia University in 1994. She currently serves as Director of The Institute for Professional Development School Studies at Towson University, a research and development initiative that focuses on improvement-oriented inquiry.

Gloria A. Neubert is Professor of Secondary Education at Towson University. She received her Ph.D. from the University of Maryland and is the author of four textbooks, three Phi Delta Kappa fastbacks, and numerous journal articles dealing with content reading and writing instruction and staff development.

Lisa A. Newcomb has been a Media Specialist with the Howard County (MD) School System for seven years. She has served as a mentor to fellow staff members by participating in Towson University's Mentoring to Master Technology Integration Project for three years and earned her Master's Degree in Instructional Technology from Towson University in 2000.

Thomas D. Proffitt is Acting Dean of the College of Education at Towson University. He holds an Ed.D. (1984) from the University of Maryland, College Park. As the former Associate Dean, he was the Coordinator of the Towson University Professional Development School Network and worked closely with the Maryland State Department of Education to develop the *Standards for Maryland Professional Development Schools*.

Jessica Wolf Rhoten was a classroom teacher for six years in a Baltimore County (MD) public school classroom and then became a Language Arts Resource Teacher for the county. She is a graduate of Towson University (B.S., Elementary Education, 1996; M.S., Reading, 2002) and is currently a full-time parent teaching her own child.

Lauren Rifkin has been a classroom teacher at the Owings Mills Elementary School/Towson University Professional Development School for the past nine years. She has also served as an Adjunct Instructor in reading and assessment for Towson University for three years. She holds a bachelor's degree from the University of Delaware and a master's degree in Reading from Towson University.

William A. Sadera is Assistant Professor of Instructional Technology in the College of Education at Towson University. His research interests focus on pre-service teacher technology preparation and the integration of the conceptual change process. He graduated with a Ph.D. in Curriculum and Instruction from Iowa State University in 2001.

Chet Scott is Principal of Owings Mills (MD) Elementary School, the first professional development school partnership with Towson University established in 1994. He holds a master's degree from Towson University and has spoken to numerous teachers, administrators, and university faculty about the added value of professional development schools for teachers and students.

Terri Wainwright is a 20-year veteran of teaching high school English. She is currently a high school mentor teacher in the Harford County (MD) Public School System, working primarily with new and untenured teachers. She also serves as Site Coordinator for the Professional Development School partnership between Towson University and Bel Air High School.

Cheryl L. Wittmann has an extensive background in the field of education in classroom, resource, and supervisory roles. She received an Ed.D. from the University of Maryland, College Park, in 1992. She currently serves as Professional Development School Facilitator for the Maryland State Department of Education, where she contributed to *Professional Development Schools: An Implementation Manual* (2003) and other publications.

David R. Wizer is currently Associate Professor at Towson University in the Department of Reading, Special Educational and Instructional Technology; and the Graduate Director of the Instructional Technology Program. He completed his Ph.D. in 1991 from the University of Maryland at College Park.

Index